I
Remember
Jimmy

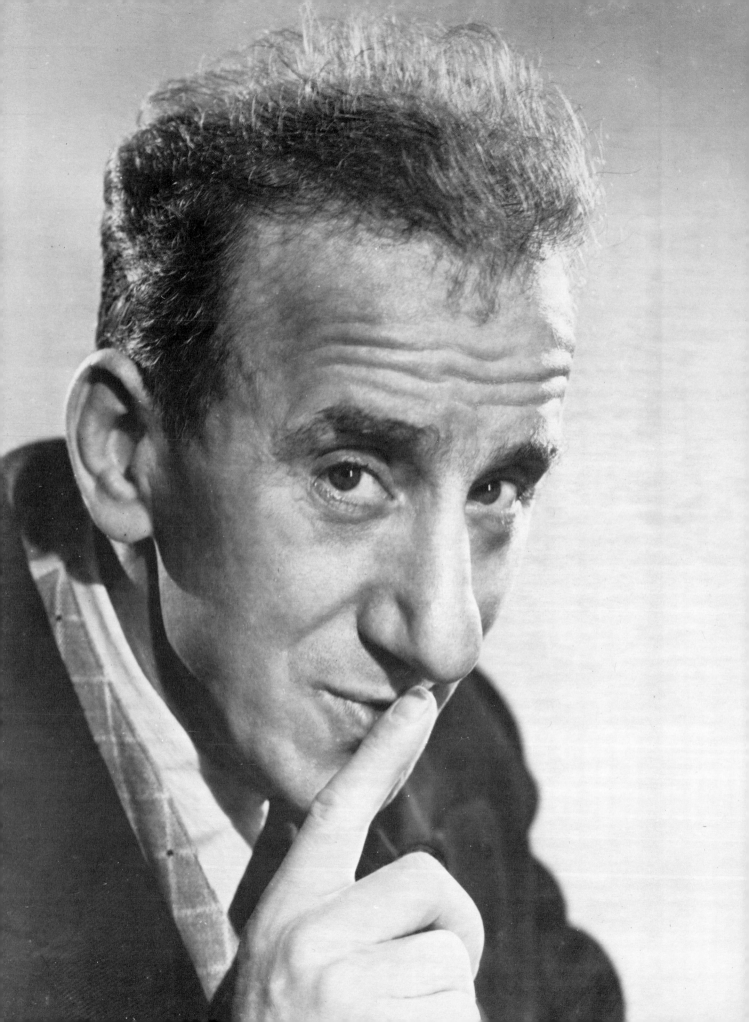

I
Remember
Jimmy

The Life and Times
of
Jimmy Durante

BY
IRENE ADLER

ARLINGTON HOUSE/PUBLISHERS

Manufactured in the United States of America.
First American Edition.

ISBN: 0-87000-483-2 HDCR.

ISBN: 0-87000-490-5 PPK.

Library of Congress Catalog Card Number: 80-67473

PHOTO CREDITS

Museum of the City of New York
p.: 6, 10, 14, 20-21, 28, 30, 34-35, 109, 132, 184-185, 186-187.

Museum of Modern Art
p.: 42, 47, 49, 59, 68, 70, 71, 72, 73, 81, 94, 96, 99, 101, 103, 106, 110, 115, 123, 127, 135, 136, 137, 138, 143, 144, 147, 148, 149, 150, 152, 155, 161, 166, 167, 177, 180, 182, 188.

UPI
p.: 17, 19, 37-38, 40, 44, 46, 50-51, 54-55, 56, 60, 61, 62, 63, 65, 67, 70, 76, 78-79, 82, 85, 96, 100, 103, 104, 105, 113, 116, 117, 118, 119, 121, 125-126, 130-131, 134, 139, 145, 151, 159, 167, 168, 169, 170, 171, 172-173, 174, 175, 176, 179, 183, 184, 185.

Contents

"When I first met Jimmy Durante, to me his nose wasn't any bigger than mine. And the more I look at him, the more I like to look at him. I know my eyesight is not bad; I can see pretty good. To me, he's handsome; and I know he's handsome to a lot of other people. Because he can walk into a dark room, and every bulb in that room can be burned out, and there's no matches, but believe me, you will feel that room light up when that face of his gets inside of it. That's my opinion of Jimmy Durante, and I've seen it happen time and time again."

Lou Clayton, Jimmy Durante's business manager and lifelong friend, was not alone in his assessment of the man affectionately known to the world as "Schnozzola." Jimmy Durante was one of America's premier entertainers for over 60 years. He was, in the truest sense, a consummate showman — a multifaceted talent whose expertise was lent to stage, screen, radio, and television in the form of his unique brand of comedy and music.

By age three, Jimmy Durante had already learned to mug for the camera, 1896.

Childhood

Jimmy Durante was born to Rosa and Bartolomeo Durante on February 10, 1893, in a three-room tenement apartment at 90 Catherine Street in New York City. Bartolomeo Durante had learned the barber's trade in Salerno, Italy, a town 30 miles southwest of Naples. In the early 1880s, he traveled to America and lived first in Brooklyn, where a neighbor, Mrs. Lentino, told him about her eligible sister Rosa back in Italy. Bartolomeo began to correspond with Rosa Lentino, and by 1886, he had saved enough money to pay for her trans-atlantic transportation. Rosa arrived on the October day when the Statue of Liberty was unveiled on Bedloe's Island and married Bartolomeo soon afterward. They had four children: Michael, Albert, Lilian, and Jimmy.

Some of Jimmy's favorite recollections of growing up were of the celebrations on the Lower East Side for holidays, election results, and important news; they were nights to remember. Bonfires were sometimes two stories high. Bartolomeo, Jimmy recalls, used to close up shop and hide his barber pole until local festivities had subsided.

As in most locales, the Fourth of July called for a major celebration. "The Fourth meant a big bonfire, street fightin' and shootin' guns, and big parades. Men rode up on horses to my dad's to get him to donate a shavin' cup. Then they'd go to the saloons and get bottles of whiskey and take a ferryboat to Staten Island for target contests in the groves. Well, these firecrackers the butcher give me, I lit a big one and it wouldn't go off. So I blow on it and bing! My brother took me to the hospital. It was a miracle I didn't go blind."

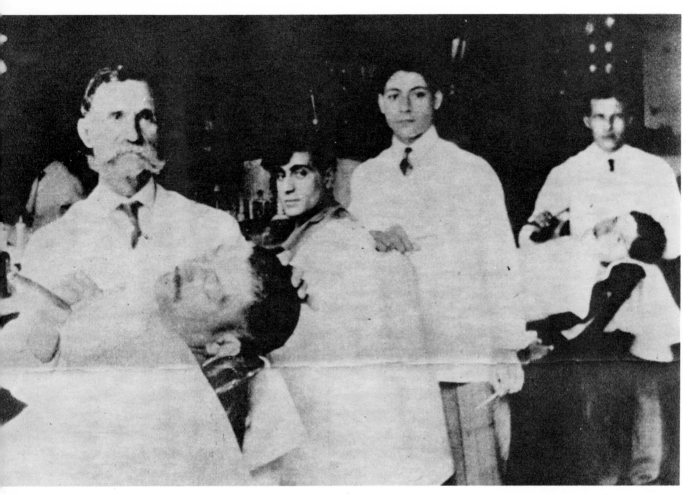

Jimmy's father, Bartolomeo (left), at work.

Jimmy's brothers Michael and Albert used to help in the barbershop by lathering the faces of their father's customers. When Jimmy turned six, he began to lend a hand. Mr. Durante planned to make him an apprentice.

In 1903, when Jimmy was ten, the Durantes moved to No. 1 Catherine Slip where they enjoyed steam heat for the first time. Jimmy took a job selling newspapers after school in City Hall Park, and New York Mayor Seth Low would send for a daily as soon as Jimmy's bellows were heard.

Jimmy left school in the eighth grade because the family needed the money he could earn from odd jobs; however, his parents did insist he study piano. He took an immediate liking to ragtime, but was ordered to learn classical music. Jimmy's teacher was Professor Fiori, a rotund Italian with a black mustache and an air of authority who demanded his students master compositions such as "Poet and Peasant," and "La Paloma." "We used to have concerts," Durante said. "You played two hands, four hands, and wore a Buster Brown collar, and had to sit with a little girl. Holy good night! How many blue notes I hit!"

Jimmy's brother Albert worked as a bookbinder's apprentice and brother Michael worked for a photoengraving firm, but most of the boys in their neighborhood had ambitions of being firemen or policemen at best. Jimmy considered a career as a policeman (Albert later spent the better part of his life as one of New York's finest) but decided to stick with "pianner playin'," although he had no theatrical ambitions at that time.

Jimmy associated with many people, but one good pal was Joey McLaughlin. "He was a kid that would inspire you. He'd say 'Go on, Jim, do this, or do that.' And with the gals of the neighborhood, he used to be a little bit of a favorite with them all. And me, they'd be around me while I was playin' pianner, you know, but they used to wind up with Joey, makin' a fuss over him and forgettin' me. It was my collosial nose and a lot of other things that made 'em winch."

Opposite the Durante barbershop was a saloon frequented by sportsmen and professional boxers. A popular referee, Florey Barnett, one day proposed a fight to Jimmy, and with a crowded barroom looking on, Jimmy foolishly accepted the challenge of facing one of Barnett's hot Brooklyn prospects, "The Kraut." The fight was held in the sports hall above the saloon. Jimmy called himself "Kid Salerno" and was knocked out in the first round.

There were frequent neighborhood dances in the Lower East Side and Jimmy got a job playing once a week for the Cherry Street Hall. His salary was 75¢ a night. Meanwhile, Jimmy continued to study classical music with Professor Fiori.

Jimmy's time with the professor was not entirely spent on music lessons, however. The professor was in love with a woman much younger than himself and wrote her many passionate letters in Italian which he demanded Jimmy translate into English. Durante also translated the young woman's letters for Fiori. But soon the woman caught on to Jimmy's role in her romance and began to fancy him over the professor. "The girl finally met me," said Jimmy. "She took one look and dropped me out of her afflictions."

One of Jimmy's many jobs was as a driver of a one-horse coal wagon. That job lasted three days; Bartolomeo would not allow his son to return home every day covered with coal dust. Jimmy next went to work at a wholesale hardware store on Chambers Street. His salary was $7.50 a week. He was an errand boy who was also in charge of the stockroom. On one occasion, Durante's co-workers became impatient for a Christmas holiday pay raise and elected Jimmy their spokesman to ask for the increase. His request appeared impudent to the boss and he was fired. Jimmy then sought the support of his colleagues, but because he had failed as a "labor leader," they wouldn't speak to him.

Jimmy then found a job as a window washer at the American Banknote Company on Broad Street, but was laid off along with other menial laborers during a corporate belt-tightening.

Ragtime Jimmy

In the spring of 1910, when Durante was 17, a friend of his suggested he visit Diamond Tony's, a Coney Island beer hall that was looking for a piano player. Jimmy went down in a turtleneck sweater and cap — his favorite dress — and landed the job at $25 a week (including tips). That was more money than the family barbershop grossed in a week.

Durante began his Coney Island career in April of 1910. The Island was by then a peninsula; the tidal creek that separated it from Brooklyn had been filled in. It was called a "nickel paradise" — a place where millions of New Yorkers bathed, picnicked, strolled the six miles of shoreline, and patronized the two great amusement parks: Fred Thompson's "Luna Park" and George Tilyou's "Steeplechase."

At the time Durante went to work at Diamond Tony's, the cafes had no orchestras and patrons were not allowed to dance. A piano was placed on a small platform and the musicians accompanied the singer-waiters and filled in with instrumentals until another singer was ready to perform. The piano players got a work break only when a fellow musician requested playing time to try out a new song. That was Jimmy's chance to get a bite to eat or play dice with some friends. The clientele of the Coney Island cafes was largely made up of prostitutes and their customers. A man would pick up a hooker on the boardwalk, take her to a cafe, and later retire with her upstairs. Jimmy played from eight o'clock each night until six in the morning, seven nights a week. It was the job at Diamond Tony's that trained Jimmy in endurance and discipline, where his famous indefatigable body and spirit were developed.

The prostitutes at Diamond Tony's took a platonic liking to Durante. Jimmy was fond of most of them and felt sorry for their miserable existences which, for most, included regular beatings from their pimp. "Some of those gals used to set beside my piano every night at Coney, and they was really crazy about me in a way, they really was. They used to come over to me with all their troubles. 'Jimmy, could you loan me five dollars? I didn't make enough tonight. And I'm scared to go back to my man.' I'd say, 'Let me talk to him, will you?' 'Oh, Jimmy, please don't. You don't understand.' So I'd draw five dollars from

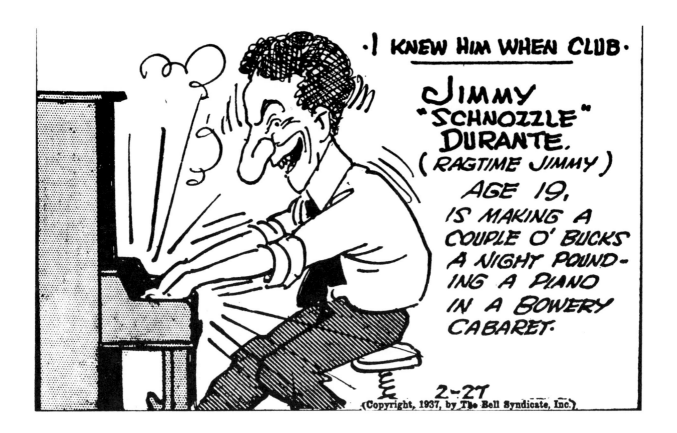

the boss and the gals would always pay it back. One wouldn't have made a dime. Maybe she hadn't eaten, or wanted a loan to go out and get something to eat, so she'd have the strength to make the money, and then she'd bring it back and give it to you.

"And down there, there used to be the most beautiful woman in the world, I thought. She used to sit next to the piano and have her drink. I don't know where she come from. Suppose we say her name was Gladie. She was 20 or maybe 19 and she was beautiful, a brunette and considered the prettiest girl on the walk. At the time she first sat down near me she had just broken up with her boyfriend — a piano player too. And she used to come into the place once in a while with this guy before they broke up, and this guy would buy wine. Boy! Buy wine at six dollars a quart, and you was a big shot when you came in there and bought wine. You know, the big sportin' men in them days used to come in and buy wine. Holy Moe! Gladie used to sit there with her man, proud as a peacock. She used to wear them big hats, with the Bird of Paradise, and rooz on her cheeks. Oh, a gal that didn't have the big hat, a hustler, was a minor leaguer.

"One night I came home early one mornin' and found my brothers waiting for me. They gave me the talkin' of my life. They said 'What's the matter with you?' 'Why,' I says to my brothers, 'I got to make some money for the house.' 'You're goin' to the dogs, kid,' my brother Albert says. And Mike, he puts in, 'What do you want to be, a souse? A pimp workin' in a dive? That's the way you're gonna wind up.' 'I don't drink. I don't chase. I'll be all right,' I tells him.

"You'd picture a piano player in them days as a bum because all you could see there in a jernt was beer or whiskey on the piano. But getting back to Gladie: she sat at the piano there and looked sometimes at my ring with the little yellow stone, not a big stone, but a nice stone that belonged to my mother. I never wanted to wear diamonds. But anyway my mother says, 'Wear it, Jimmy.' I don't know, it must have been worth a couple of hundred, bought on time like everything else we had. Gladie liked little melodies, and I used to play them for her. I really liked her. She was a hell of a lovely gal, and one night she says, 'Jimmy, can I borrow your ring?' I gives it to her, but she doesn't come back the next night.

"Every night for two weeks I watch the door for her. I'm getting nervous, but at last she comes in. And what do you think happened? She hocked it to pay for a certain kind of operation. I asked if I could take her home some night. I was just a kid. What the hell. I was in love with her. I'd thought I was in love before, but this was different. One night she came into Diamond Tony's and my heart lit up and I played some songs she always asked for, but when I turned and looked at her she said, 'I don't want to see you no more, Jimmy. I'm back with my man. And I don't ever want to see you no more.' "

Jimmy was brokenhearted, but hurt for him was never accompanied by anger or resentment, only sadness and the hope of a brighter future. "I left Diamond Tony's for the Chatham Club in New York's Chinatown. It was only five blocks from where I lived. I says to myself, 'This is a tonier jernt; maybe Gladie will come up here.' She did travel around."

The Chatham Club was a real hot-spot. Irving Berlin once worked there, and New York's toughest gangsters used the hall as their hangout. All night long Durante banged out Tin Pan Alley favorites. "At three in the morning down there in Chinatown it was like Broadway and 42nd Street. I made more money at the Chatham Club than I've made in any jernt until I went in with my partners Eddie Jackson and Lou Clayton. The entertainers used to split up two or three hundred in tips.

"One night, who should walk in, but Gladie. Must have been about four in the mornin'. Gladie was with her sweetheart, a new one, and they got on the floor to dance. The Chatham used to close their doors at one o'clock, put the tables aside, and dance all night. There was no dancin' allowed in the cafes in them days, but they danced at the Chatham irregardless. Well, my heart jumped when Gladie came in. I played one of the melodies she always liked. But she just turned her head away, without even a hello or how-do-you-do. Gee, it broke my heart. I'd smile and look at her, but every time her head would go the other way."

One of Durante's acquaintances at the Chatham was "Slicker," a pickpocket who hung out at the club until the early morning rush hour when he'd take to the streets to begin "work." Jimmy recalls that one day "I went downstairs to kid around with a fellow named Charlie Daw and at the end of the bar there was a phone and Slicker was talkin' on the phone to his sweetheart, and he says, 'Listen' — and you know how some things stick out in your mind and you remember the dialogue — and this fellow Slicker says, 'Listen, I got to see you tonight. If you don't see me, I'm gonna shoot myself right in the head. You don't believe it? You don't believe it! You don't, huh?' And now he's hysterical. So help me, I see him pull a gun right out of his pocket and shoot himself right in the head, topple over — but he lived. He is in the hospital for a year, I think. The bullet goes right over his brain, I guess. And it makes me think of the torch I am carrying for Gladie. And it makes me afraid to be in love.''

The next summer, Jimmy went back to Coney Island and worked at Kerry Walsh's, a place across the street from Diamond Tony's. There he met a young singer named Eddie Cantor. They hit it off right away. ''Eddie and me had lots of fun, the two of us. We seemed to match. If a guy would ask for a song, and we didn't know the song, we'd make one up on the spot. If a guy wanted 'The Hills of Kentucky,' which I didn't know or ever heard of, I'd fake a melody and Eddie would sing, 'The Hills of Kentucky are far, far away, and when you're from them hills, you're away from them hills, yes, away from them Hills of Kentucky.' So the guy who had asked us for the song and slipped us a couple of bucks for it would object: 'What the hell did you sing to me?' Then Eddie would say, 'Why, the Hills of Kentucky.' Then the guy would say, 'What? That ain't the words.' And Eddie would say, innocent-like, 'Are there two of them? Well, gee, I'll ask the piano player does he know the other one?' And then we'd go on from there, and we'd make a regular routine of it and Eddie would say to the man, 'Oh,' he'd say, 'you must mean this one.' And he'd sing the title right in the guy's kisser and I'd follow him on the piano: 'Old Kentucky in the hills, which we love so dear . . . ' And the guy would yell his brains out, 'Stop it! That's not it, either.' He'd say, 'What are you guys, wise guys?' Eddie, with his big brown eyes, would shed real tears and sob. 'No,' he'd say, 'and if you want the money back, we'll give you the money back.' But as he says this he's walkin' away from the guy. The money is in his shoe already, and the guy wants his money back; but Eddie walks away too fast. What a guy that Eddie! He's tops!''

Cantor and Durante continued to remain good friends, and it was Eddie who first encouraged Jimmy to begin talking to the audience while playing the piano. ''Piano playing is going to get you nothing,'' said Cantor. ''You'll be a piano player till you're a hundred years old. You gotta look further than that. People like you a whole lot. So why don't you get up on the floor and say something to the people? Make remarks while you're playing the piano.''

''Gee, Eddie,'' Durante said, ''I wouldn't do that. I'd be afraid people would laugh at me.''

''Ragtime Jimmy,'' as he was known then, had played piano in as many as 20 places by 1915. That was the year that Maxine's, a rowdy Brooklyn cafe that employed Durante, was closed by the police. ''Maxine's was so tough,'' Jimmy explained, ''that if you took off your hat you was a sissy.''

Eddie Cantor (left) and Jimmy Durante.

Durante pounded the New York pavement until he got a tip that there was work available at the Alamo, a cabaret in Harlem on 125th Street between Seventh and Eighth Avenues. It had two rooms, one with a bar and another with tables, both dimly lit.

"I landed the job at the Alamo, and I got $45 a week and tips for playing from eight o'clock at night until I was subconscious." A month after starting at the Alamo, Durante became the leader of the five-piece band.

When cabaret dancing became legal, and Durante began to realize that there was big money to be made from the freely spending gangster crowd, he attempted to step away from the piano for the first time in his career, but was ordered to make such appearances brief by Mr. Sakerson, the boss. When the Alamo management bought a Coney Island club, called the College Arms, Durante began to work in both clubs.

Also in 1915, Eddie Jackson, a high-silk-hat cakewalker and baritone, and his vaudeville partner Eddie Murray auditioned for Durante at the Alamo. They failed to make the grade, but this meeting was the beginning of a lifelong relationship. Jackson, born of Jewish parents in Brooklyn, was three years younger than Durante. He, too, had only an eighth grade education. Before entering vaudeville, Jackson had worked in a bookbindery in the Bush Terminal Building in Brooklyn. His foreman was a young, slim, Italian lad named Al Capone. Capone made $18 a week, Jackson, $8. Al played the horses but not very well. In fact, he often borrowed money from Jackson to support his gambling. While continuing at the bindery, Eddie began his show business career as a singing waiter in Canarsie, Brooklyn, and with the double income could afford to lend Capone some change every now and then. When the bookbinders struck for higher wages, Jackson left, but Capone didn't forget his pal. Years later, when the Chicago mobster visited New York nightclubs to see Jackson, he would toss $100 bills at Eddie.

In 1917, Durante auditioned Jackson again — this time with Miss Dot Taylor, a blues singer. Jimmy booked their act for the Alamo, and when Miss Taylor left that winter, Jackson stayed on at the club. He also stayed with Durante for more than 60 years.

"Those were great days," Eddie Jackson recalls, "and the competition was terrific. We had no microphones anywhere, and you had to score every time in those noisy joints. That old school of singers had timing. Like Jolson and Sophie Tucker. They could put over songs. Jimmy always picked out my songs for me. He has an uncanny instinct for the right ones, and he is a great accompanist. He has a genius for tempo, never too fast or too slow. He keeps heating you up, and when you go on the floor with that man, you're in. He never tries to steal the show, always shares the glory, which he has plenty of. I don't read music, and Jimmy teaches the melody to me. He works awful hard, and he's serious about it."

Dixieland jazz was the rage of 1917, so Jimmy hired several musicians from New Orleans. Johnny Stien, a drummer, and Archie Baquet, a great clarinet player, and formed "Jimmy Durante's New Orleans Jazz Band." "Our band was a riot. On the level. From all over the country they used to come to hear our music. It was my first big billin'."

"Jimmy Durante's New Orleans Jazz Band" at the Alamo Club, New York, 1915.

Jeanne

During the winter of 1918, a young woman from the Midwest, Maude Jeanne Olson, wandered into the Alamo to seek employment as a singer. She auditioned for Jimmy that evening and was booked at the Alamo for a short stay. She remained with Jimmy for the rest of her life.

Jeanne Olson was born in Toledo, Ohio, but had lived most of her young adulthood in Detroit. Her parents were divorced, and she was raised by her grandmother. Jeanne sang soprano in midwestern vaudeville houses and decided to try to make it in show business in New York where she happened to meet a kindly restaurateur and booking agent, Sigmund Werner (he had given Rudolph Valentino his first job as a dancer). Jeanne spent her Sundays with the Werner family, and all in all, life was made considerably easier with their help.

Jeanne was in her late twenties when she auditioned for Durante. He was initially hesitant to hire her, but her charm probably persuaded him more than anything else. "Sopranos and violins always seemed a little bit sissy. We wanted noise, brasses, drums, and piano." But then Jeanne playfully insulted Jimmy's musicianship. His response: "Dem's the conditions that prevail."

He later recalled, "She didn't make me mad when she panned my pianner playin'. I had to laugh. When we finished work, we used to go have a little bite to eat, and I'd drop her off at the door of her roomin' house, and I was really crazy 'bout her."

One afternoon Jimmy invited Jeanne to the Hippodrome theater to see a show. Neither of them had ever seen a play or musical and both were excited about going. Durante met Jeanne at the corner of 43rd Street and Sixth Avenue in his usual turtleneck and cap.

"Are you going to the show with me like that?" Jeanne asked angrily.

"Why sure, who else?" She turned and walked away.

"Daniel Boom wore a cap!" Jimmy called out.

"For the life of me, I couldn't understand it. I had got tickets in the orchestra, too. I tore 'em up and walked away. So after that, anytime I met her, I had a necktie on, and I never wore a cap again, which I found out to be the right thing to do when you go out, not to wear a cap or a sweater. Down in the neighborhood where I was born in, believe it or not, some people went through their whole life without ever leavin' the neighborhood and never seein' a show. I don't think my own mother, Lord have mercy on her soul, ever left any neighborhood once she moved into it. They had their motion pictures around there, the nickelodeons, and the little dances in the neighborhood. On the East Side, the Democratic Social Club had a dance, the St. James Church had a dance: that was their form of entertainment.''

Near the Alamo was a burlesque house where Toodles Z. Lemay, a gin-guzzling stripper, worked. She frequented the Alamo and often spoke with Jimmy. Jeanne became jealous of their flirtation.

''Who's your friend? From the Vanderbilts?'' Jeanne would ask sarcastically.

''Naw,'' said Jim, ''just a gal who is a good customer.''

''What's she drinking there? Water? You going out with her tonight?''

''Oh, I take her home once in a while.'' Jimmy then tried to kiss Jeanne.

She pushed him away and sarcastically asked, ''What are you, a two-timer?''

''You know, I can fire you.''

''Then why don't you?''

''Aw, I guess I'll let you stay another week.''

When Durante used to take Jeanne around the corner for a bite to eat, Eddie Jackson and the troupe would often go along. ''We would be sittin' ten at a table and havin' coffee, cakes, and scrambled eggs. So I'd say, 'Now, Eddie, I'm goin' out with Jeanne alone tonight, but I don't want nobody to know about it but you.' Then I'd say, 'Eddie, wave your hand when I get to the cashier's desk and everyone will think I'm goin' home alone. Jeanne will come outside later to meet me on the sly.' So I'd walk up to the desk and I'd tell the boss that the fellow that's goin' to wave his hand, it's a signal that he's goin' to pay the check. So Eddie would wave his hand, and when he came out, he'd get stuck. And after a few times of that, Eddie never waved his hand no more, even to this day, in a restaurant.''

Jimmy recalled that Jeanne, like himself, would occasionally indulge in flirtation. ''There was an airplane flyer living at the apartment house where Jeanne lived. This fellow would take her out for coffee, you know, take her out for breakfast. And when I'd see Jeanne again I'd make like as if I ain't disturbed about it, so I'd just ask her questions, like, 'Where was you? Did you enjoy yourself?' And then when she'd toss her head, I'd say against my will, 'I like him. He's a nice fellow.' So she'd say at length, 'Yes, I had a lovely time. Grand time.' She'd build it up and up and then she'd say, 'Good night.' And I'd say, 'What's your hurry?' And she'd torment me with, 'Well, you're busy with your business. By the way, how's your seidel-of-gin girlfriend?' Then I'd say I was only trying to be courteous to Miss Lemay, and Jeanne, she'd snort and say, 'Well, you can't play both ends in the middle.' Oh gee, I sure was in love with Jeanne!''

Sigmund Werner's daughter Jenice recalls Jeanne saying that Jimmy walked like a chimpanzee. "She used to fall in behind him and imitate him, but he did not know this until years afterward. She was mad about him."

During the winter of 1920, Jeanne suffered severe abdominal pains. "Mr. Werner used to go with her from doctor to doctor," Jimmy recalled, "and then her mother came east, and later she was operated on. Her mother, Mary, was married to a Mr. Joseph Blenman. Jeanne liked her mother real well, and I liked her father. She had a brother, Earl Olson, who'd been gassed during the [First] World War. There wasn't much difference in their ages." Jeanne was committed to Flower Hospital and was successfully operated on. When she was well enough to travel, she returned to Detroit for a short vacation with her family.

"While Jeanne was gone those weeks, we started correspondin' on close terms, and I would call her 'Toots' and she would call me 'Tootis.' And that's what we called each other all the time. She was a smart girl. Aw, what a smart girl! And a great inspiration for me."

New Year's Day, 1921, was a sad day for Jimmy. His mother had been ill for some time and Jimmy had spent many hours at her bedside, but on January 1st, she died.

Jimmy proposed marriage to Jeanne upon her return from Detroit. They were married on June 19, 1921, in St. Malachy's Catholic Church on West 49th Street; Jimmy was 28, Jeanne, 29. Jeanne wore a brown taffeta dress that she had spent the entire wedding eve altering. "It was a flowered dress," remembered Jenice Werner, "and Jeanne had a large picture hat, brown, and brown shoes to go with it. Jimmy's favorite color is brown, and I think it's because Jeanne wore brown the day they were married. I remember that she sewed this dress first with her left hand and then with her right. She was ambidextrous, and we laughed because she sewed so quickly and so well. We laughed about other things, like certain words she would hesitate over. She had a bit of a French accent too, because her grandma, Mrs. Peel, was a French-Canadian."

The Durantes wedding party was held at South Beach on Staten Island. Jimmy's father, Bartolomeo liked Jeanne very much and she was fond of him. Along with the guests, they enjoyed games on the beach, Italian food, red wine, then music and dancing. The following night, Jimmy returned to work at the Alamo — without his wife.

"I figured 24 hours together would spoil the marriage. And in most cases I think it is the truth. If a party is 24 hours together with each other, well, naturally I'd get on her nerves and she'd get on my nerves. And I've got an awful bad habit: instead of tellin' the truth, so as not to harm nobody I tell them little lies; you know, like not tellin' Jeanne I'm playin' cards with the boys. So I tell Jeanne I worry about her health if she works, when all the time I just don't want her to work because I'm old fashioned. And it was a big mistake to kill off a talent like Jeanne's as things later turned out."

The Durantes moved first into a single furnished room on 23rd Street. Later they moved to 95th Street where they shared a kitchen and bathroom with a doctor. Jeanne objected to that arrangement, so they moved again, this time to West 52nd Street where they had extra rooms which Jeanne rented out because the $125 a month rent was too much for Jimmy to pay. Their first tenant was Jack Roth, Durante's new drummer.

Jeanne was instrumental in propelling Jimmy's career forward. First she urged him to demand more money from the Alamo. Then, after his salary was raised to $57 a week, she encouraged him to quit, to "take a big step. You are too big for that place," she told her husband.

In October 1921, Jimmy quit the Alamo and he went to work in Brooklyn, in a cafe underneath the Orpheum Theatre. Some months later, he landed his first job on "The Avenue" — at the Nightingale Club on 48th Street and Broadway — and became the leader of a six-piece band. Jimmy was excited to be breaking into the "big circle." He performed in a tuxedo for the first time; he even learned how to loop a bow tie, and he became totally engrossed in his newfound notoriety.

"I'm down at the Nightingale. They're not all a bunch of angels, including me. There's a little gal down there by the name of Rose. You know, sometimes whether you mean anythin' by it, it's just a flirtation, nothin' serious in it, but sometimes that's the root of things. This little gal down there, I am foolin' around with a little bit, and Jeanne happens to find out about it. Brother! Well, we used to get a lot of tips down there in the Nightingale. After work I'd be flirtin' around with this little gal, and I'd be home late, and I'd say I'd be workin' extra down at my old pal Jimmy Kelly's place on Sullivan Street. The tips that I used to get from the Nightingale, I'd say this is the money I am getting from Kelly's. Another one of them little lies. After a couple of weeks, Jeanne finds out the truth, and she is very much put out and I don't blame her. Believe me, she was a sincere girl. She was very, very sincere. I told her, 'Jeanne, there's nothin' to it, believe me, there's nothin' to it.' Anyway, I quit seein' the gal any more. And Jeanne is one strict gal, and she wants me home after work. That is one of the main things. She is alone all night, and she insists that I come home, and I think it is no more than right; and anyone will tell you, from then on, after I finish work I used to go home every night."

Durante continued to arrive home in the early hours of the morning, however, and Jeanne continued to grow gradually more despondent. "I should have let her go back to work as a singer, but how am I to know the future," said Jimmy.

As the novelty of working on Broadway gave way to routine, Jimmy set his sights, as Eddie Cantor had urged, beyond piano playing. Still with no thought of being an actor or comedian, he set about becoming a songwriter. His first sincere effort was a collaboration with Chris Smith on a ragtime song called "Daddy, Your Mama Is Lonesome for You." After Jeanne sang the song for the Triangle Music Company, they bought it outright for $100. Then Smith and Durante wrote "I've Got My Habits On," which was also purchased and ultimately netted Jimmy nearly $1,500 in royalties — the first big money he ever saw.

In the summer of 1922, Jimmy worked in New York State's Catskill mountain resort area of Green Lake. Jeanne wanted to be with him, but Jimmy insisted she visit her mother and stepfather on the West Coast. The Durantes had, by then, purchased a small house in Flushing, New York, and Jimmy was trying to save as much of his salary as he could for the mortgage payments.

Enter Lou Clayton

By the autumn of 1922, there were several thousand speakeasies in New York City, and Frank Nolan, one of Jimmy's co-workers at the Nightingale, suggested to Durante that he open his own club. Jimmy didn't like the idea at first, but when a successful bootlegger offered him a loan of $700 to set up shop, Durante agreed. "I'll go in on one condition," he said. "Hot or cold, I want seventy-five a week. And if we don't do business, let's close up the place the first week I don't get my seventy-five."

The Club Durant (the "e" in Durante was mistakenly omitted from the donated electric sign) opened in late autumn of 1923. One night, a few months later, Lou Clayton, a soft-shoe dancer, stopped by the club. Clayton would later become Durante's best friend.

Clayton was born Louis Finkelstein in Brooklyn in 1887. He came from a very poor family and, as a boy, sold newspapers by the streetcars. One day he slipped and fell under the wheels of a moving trolley. Although he was crippled for years afterward, his determination was indomitable. Exercise and will power overcame his lameness, and by 1919, he was the star dancer of the Orpheum Theatre in San Francisco.

Durante was introduced to Clayton at his table in the club and after a little conversation, Jimmy asked Lou if he'd like to come into the business. Lou asked Durante how much he could make. About a hundred a week, said Durante. Clayton was used to making closer to fifteen hundred a week and had to turn the offer down. A few days later, though, Clayton and Durante ran into each other on the street, and Lou asked Jimmy exactly what his role in the new speakeasy would be.

"Well," said Durante, "I'll tell you, Lou. We've got a partner by the name of Harry Harris. You know the people who are comin' to this place, they're not strait-laced fellows. They're fellows who are runnin' liquor mostly. And when a fellow comes in with a girl, this Harris leans over and starts singin' 'The Oregon Trail Is Where I Found You' or 'Melancholy Baby' or one of them blues songs — and this Harris never looks at the fellow whatsoever. He keeps lookin' at the girl, and he keeps lookin' in the girl's eyes, or at her busts the whole time. I'm scared one of them fellows some of these nights is goin' to get

liquor in him, or flit or somethin', and he'll shoot this fellow Harris right between his two eyes. Rather than have some inflection befoul us, I'd just as leave get him out of the place, buy him out.''

''How much does your place cost?'' asked Clayton.

''Well, it now stands us around $10,000,'' was the response.

''Well, Jimmy, what would my end be?''

''Twenty-five per cent. But I don't want you to put up no cash, Lou. The rest of us will buy the fellow out and you can have twenty-five per cent of the place if you only just come in with us. You dance like nobody's business, and I know you'll do us nothin' but good.''

''Jim, I'd want to feel as if I was coming in on an even footing. And I'm not coming in as a bully or a tough guy, and if I take twenty-five per cent, I'd just like to put up my end.''

''That suits me.''

''Further and more,'' continued Clayton, ''if I do come in, I want you to know that I'm going to be president, and I'm going to be treasurer, too.''

''That's good enough for me,'' said Durante. ''You can handle the money. All I want to do is play pianner.''

''Jimmy, I'm gonna give you $2,500, my end, and I'm stepping in and opening with you this coming Thursday night.''

''I want to make it very plain and emphatic,'' Clayton said just before his death in 1950, ''that during all those years of our association and partnership, there wasn't a piece of paper written between Durante and myself. There never has been a contract. We have cut up millions of dollars. Never at any time did Jimmy ever ask me for a contract, and at no time did I ever ask Jimmy for a scrap of paper to show our association together. He knew the ethics as I did, and that it was by the nod of our heads we did our business. One time Jimmy gave me a picture of himself, and on that picture, which I treasure dearly, he inscribed on it ahead of his signature the only contract you might say that we ever had: 'To my dear pal and partner, Lou, until death do we part.' ''

The positive presence of Lou Clayton influenced the club's success almost immediately. Lou was strong willed; he never backed away from anything, which was just the kind of personality they needed to succeed. Jimmy, on the other hand, tried to please everyone, and got himself into all sorts of jams. Phil Silvers once described Lou and Jimmy's relationship as that of a father and a son. Clayton was six years older than Durante and was much more mature and wise. He was, at times, severely critical of Jimmy, but he allowed no one else to be.

Clayton even handled customer trouble with street-wise, firm diplomacy. And if the diplomacy didn't work, he'd slip a rowdy a Mickey Finn — an alcoholic beverage laced with a drug guaranteed to dull the senses. Clayton later recalled, ''I got the reputation of being the best Mickey Finn giver in New York City.''

It was Clayton who first got Durante to leave his piano and stand on stage. Another piano player was hired, and Jimmy began to sing his songs and inject funny material into his act. The routine called for Durante's friend Eddie Jackson to stand at one end of the room and sing along with him. Then Lou would saunter over to Jimmy on stage, Eddie would make his way up, and then the three of them would begin to sing and improvise jokes. Clayton popularized Durante's nickname ''Schnozzola'' during their spontaneous routines. (Sime Silverman, editor of *Variety*, had coined the name.)

Durante described one of the routines: ''Clayton ran out of the kitchen pretendin' to look for me, and when he found me, he would grab me by the beak and yell that he has discovered oil. Then Jackson would ask where, and Clayton would say, 'In Jimmy's Schnozz!' Then Jackson would grab me by the nose, and then little by little we graduated, got bits here and there, and added to our routine. I wrote songs the first year like 'Jimmy, The Well Dressed Man,' and afterward, 'I Ups to Him and He Ups to Me,' and 'Who'll Be With You When I'm Far Away?' ''

(Durante often talked about his nose. ''I get hunneds of letters from long-nosed people thankin' me for puttin' da schnozzola where it belongs.'' For a time, he even had his nose insured with Lloyd's of London for $100,000. An impression of the famous ''schnozz'' is enshrined on the concrete walkway in front of Mann's Chinese Theatre in Hollywood alongside casts of Betty Grable's legs, Mary Pickford's hands, Charlie Chaplin's feet, and other renowned appendages.)

A 1929 caricature of Durante.

The Good Years

Clayton, Jackson, and Durante were spending almost every minute of their lives together during those early days of their partnership. Jeanne could not complain about Lou Clayton as an associate of Jimmy's because of the Club Durant's rapid rise to popularity, which he had engineered, and his scrupulous honesty. But she found herself more alone and more depressed, and she began to drink.

The Durantes had bought their first car, paid off the mortgage on their house, and Jeanne had everything she had ever dreamed of — except her husband. She was scared being in the house alone and began calling Jimmy at the club. She'd even go so far as to lock herself in the bedroom and call him whenever she had to go to the bathroom. Jimmy would stay on the line until she returned safely to bed. Sometimes these calls would interrupt Durante in the middle of one of his routines, which added to a growing unhappiness in the marriage.

Jeanne was sickly to begin with, and jealous, and with Jimmy away from home for most of every day, she became desperate. She begged Jimmy to give it all up and move to California. But he felt he belonged to the public and while he loved his wife, he could not effectively integrate her into the life he wanted for himself. He had, at one time, thought about hiring her as his business advisor, but when the crackerjack Clayton came along, that was ruled out. And not once did Jimmy guess that Jeanne had a secret desire to sing at his club. He didn't feel his wife should work in any case, "and that," again said Durante, "was the biggest mistake I ever made."

Meanwhile, Durante's talents as a stage performer were developing rapidly. The team of Clayton, Jackson, and Durante became the talk of Broadway. Sime Silverman gave the trio a lot of free publicity in his widely read *Variety* column. He called them "The Three Sawdust Bums." "There is no act in the business that grows on an audience like these three boys," he wrote. George M. Cohan visited the club. Stars of Broadway shows dropped by after their performances. Many show business playwrights and columnists frequented the place.

Club Durant became wildly successful even though its owners hired no publicity agent and refused to pay for police protection. The entertainment was of such high caliber that the place was continuously crowded until well after sunrise. Often, known murderers like Legs Diamond and Mad Dog Coll would show up; Durante and Jackson would leave the premises when they saw those men. Clayton stayed to check their firearms and see that no one got rowdy.

Under normal conditions, though, the club ran smoothly. When Clayton and Durante recognized a couple walking in, they would break into song: "Skeet, skat, skat, skoo. Here come some friends of mine. Sit them down at table nine. See that they don't buy no wine." At other times, the two jokers would each grab a person and escort them to widely separate tables. Once seated himself, Durante would look perplexed and say, "What happened? I come in with a girl!" And while everybody laughed, the couple would be reunited at some center table.

The jokes at the Club Durant were always made in the spirit of good clean fun — never off-color or embarrassing to the clientele. And the entertainment was continuous. "They constitute the best entertainment in New York," wrote critic Gilbert Seldes. "I doubt if a greater combination ever lived," added Damon Runyon.

"We made what to us was laughter all the time," Clayton later said. "We wanted to keep you in the mood. When we got tired and felt we wanted to get off the floor, the orchestra, which we later enlarged to twelve pieces, would play. It was intimate fun. You were right up against one another. You'd come in at eleven o'clock and leave at seven o'clock the next morning. You wouldn't know where the night flew by, because at no time was there a lull in the place, and that's how we got sayings like 'There's a lull in the place. What happened? The piano must be busted!' And those things were cues, and we'd start doing something. Eddie'd get out there and start singing a song. Or I'd get out there and fly across the floor. We never stole the play from one another while a partner was doing his turn. We knew how to build each other up."

As the club flourished, so too did Jeanne's resentment — not of Jimmy's success per se, but of how show business was dominating virtually all of her husband's time. Years later, Lou Clayton discussed his involvement in the situation: "Jeanne didn't care anything about the money. [Jimmy was making nearly $2,000 a week.] She just wanted the companionship of Jimmy. And I don't blame her or any other woman, because that companionship from a man of that kind is beautiful.

"And I know this woman at first tried to like me; but I lost what I wouldn't call affection, but her friendship. What I mean is, she would never abuse me, and never do anything to hurt me, but when I would see her, I would love to walk over to her and exchange salutations. But she'd always ignore me. Well, I'm the type of man, if you ignore me once, I'll try to repeat what I said. But if you ignore me again, why, I will just take it for granted that you do not want me to talk to you, and I will not talk to you anymore. And that woman never spoke to me but one time again. I don't think Jeanne spoke to me but once in fifteen years. I finally asked her, 'Jeanne, why don't you be friends with me? Did I do something?' And she looked at me, hurt and bitter, and said, 'You took my love away from me.'

"Jeanne didn't want money or sables or any big cars. She was not a greedy woman. She'd have been tickled to death if Jimmy was making $50 a week, just so he'd stay home with her. She really adored her man. But she blamed me for his success. When I tell you that I lost her respect and friendship, it hurt me. And good women always get plenty hurt when they marry men who belong to the whole world.

"When Jeanne started to drink, it was because it was the only way she could give vent to her feelings. She was so alone, and you know what this show business is. When you become a success in it, you become a servant of the public. No time is your own. When Jeanne did go out in public with Jimmy, when they went to a restaurant or to the theater, someone would walk over to Jimmy Durante, compliment him, slap him on the back, touch his nose or shake hands with him, or ask for an autograph. And Jeanne always felt that that was time taken away from her. That was her time, and she wanted it. There comes an hour in every person's life when he or she wants to be alone with some loved person, and if anyone steps on that hour, he or she is an intruder. And that's the way it seemed to Jeanne Durante with her Jimmy. She resented it very, very much."

At one point, Jeanne tried to get her husband to take an interest in community activities. She sponsored afternoon get-togethers with local friends, but Jimmy was too exhausted during the day and made a poor host. This intensified Jeanne's sense of futility. From her point of view, she met defeat at every turn.

The Durantes spent the summer of 1925 vacationing in California and tensions between them eased. While there, Jeanne begged Jimmy to forsake Broadway and remain on the West Coast, but he wouldn't agree to that. In September, they returned to New York where Durante faced another problem: unbeknownst to Jimmy, a man he'd given an alcoholic drink to in the club was a federal agent. For violating the Prohibition Amendment, Club Durant was padlocked.

A few weeks after the club was closed, Lou Clayton crossed paths with an old friend "the Quaker," who owned the Dover Club on 51st Street and Sixth Avenue. He wanted Clayton, Jackson, and Durante to headline in his nightclub. Clayton asked for $3,000 a week. The Quaker explained that $3,000 was their average take; the best he could offer was $1,750 plus 50 per cent of all club revenue over $10,000. Clayton agreed, and the first week of their appearance, the Dover Club grossed over $17,000. When Clayton saw that, he demanded 60 per cent of the club, thereby becoming its principal owner. So great was the drawing power of "The Three Sawdust Bums" that the Quaker gladly relinquished his ownership of the place for a 40 per cent interest. The name Dover remained, and Clayton, Jackson, and Durante became the new management. The team continued to work long hours, seven nights a week. "It wasn't all easy sailing," recalled Clayton. "It was a tough life, a rough life. But we liked every minute of it. I was good and strong then. And Jimmy was strong. And we had our youth, and we could stand it. But now that we've learned what life is, I don't think you print enough money for us to go through it again."

(Left to right) *Jackson, Durante, and Clayton — "The Three Sawdust Bums."*

While the trio was working the Dover Club, the famous Palace Theatre expressed a desire to book them for a week. Clayton demanded $3,000; the Palace turned them down. They stayed with the Dover until a series of speakeasy-type disturbances involving gangsters, police, prostitutes, and federal agents began to discourage the men and affect their performances. As principal owners, it was their job to maintain order as well as entertain, and by late 1926, the strain became overwhelming. In January 1927, Clayton, Jackson, and Durante signed to play the Parody Club on East 48th Street — they were each paid $1,000 a week, with no interest in the club, but a promise of a higher salary if business improved. After a couple of weeks at the Parody, they received a salary increase and terrific reviews, but most important, they heard from the Shuberts, Florenz Ziegfeld, the Palace Theatre, the Loew's State Theatre, and others — all asking for appearances by the hottest team in town.

"The price is five grand now," announced Clayton to all comers. Jimmy begged him to accept the $3,500 the Palace was offering, but Lou told him to "be a good boy and shut up. You tend to the joke department, and Eddie to his singing. I'll look after the business end."

Word got to Clayton one night at the Parody that Fanny Brice had fallen ill and had to withdraw from her Palace Theatre engagement. Sensing an opportunity to play at the theater that symbolized the best in vaudeville, Clayton challenged the Palace: if his trio did not break the house record, the Palace wouldn't owe them a dime. If they did, $5,500 a week was his price. The Palace agreed.

They broke the record set by Beatrice Lilly in their first week; they were held over for three weeks. "We was collosial," said Durante. "The Sawdust Bums" appeared frequently at the Palace for the next two years to consistently packed houses. This was quite a feat for a vaudeville act considering that motion picture "talkies" were emerging and were beginning to draw audiences away from live entertainment.

It was during their Palace appearances that Clayton, Jackson, and Durante perfected their famous "wood act." Lou would comment that Jimmy was a blockhead. Durante replied that he was overjoyed to learn this because wood was the most valuable thing on earth. Then Jimmy would sing his original song extolling the wonders of wood while Clayton and Jackson brought out sundry wooden articles. Boards, curtain rods, furniture, picture frames, violins, and even an outhouse were laboriously collected and piled high on the stage.

On Memorial Day 1928, Clayton was approached by the agent for a string of midwestern theaters. For $5,500 a week, the boys agreed to go on tour to Cincinnati, Chicago, and Milwaukee. They not only had a wonderful time charming audiences in those three metropolitan areas, but they learned a show business lesson as well.

Durante described the circumstances which involved a detour to Minneapolis: "There was this act on ahead of us called 'The Cowboy and the Girl.' Now, I'm standin' in the wings and they got lines like 'Roses are red, violets are blue, horses neck, do you?' And this act was gettin' dynamite laughs. And so we were in high spirits, and I go out there. I look down at George Burns and Gracie Allen (who were in Minneapolis at the time) and they applaud like mad, but we get little applause from anyone else. And then I open with 'I'm Jimmy the Well Dressed Man.' Believe me, in all the years I been in the business, nothin', just nothin' happened. I got on a raccoon coat, and I remember hearin' someone in the audience sayin' out loud, 'He ain't well-dressed!'

"And then we do 'I Know Darn Well I Can Do Without Broadway,' and I come to a line where Shubert is supposed to be standin' in the wings, and he comes out and says, 'Jimmy, put in both knees, and Jolson goes!' It got nothin! And that was out biggest laugh in New York.

"Now we're discouraged. Jackson didn't go so good with his number, either. Lou got some applause for his dancin' but everythin' was kind of sour and we go off. Well, Burns and Allen are awful good people and they come to our dressin' room and they simply got to laugh about this. They had done well, and they always did do well. [Afterward,] around the bookin' offices in New York, every time Lou would show up, the booker would say, 'Do you want us to book you in Minneapolis?'

An early publicity photo.

To Durante's immediate right are Joe E. Brown and Ethel Merman.

"We hadn't given them what they wanted. It was before the big broadcastin' days, and sound was just comin' into da movies, and I found out that Broadway and New York ain't the whole world. There's a great big country outside of it, and each place has a solid humor of its own and you've got to have an act that is right down to earth. It wasn't the fault of Minneapolis. It was our fault. And I was very happy in 1934 when Minneapolis voted me the best comedian in pictures. I loved 'em for this. I loved 'em for teaching me a valuable lesson."

Back in New York, Clayton, Jackson, and Durante played Les Ambassadeurs. They appeared there for only a season, but during their stay, they performed with Ethel Zimmerman, a girl who had been trying to break into the big time for quite a while. She sang nights at an obscure cafe, Little Russia, and worked days as a secretary for a Wall Street broker. Clayton and Durante auditioned and hired her for $85 a week. Clayton suggested she change her name, which she did — to Merman — and the powerhouse singer stayed in the trio's act for a couple of months before moving on to her own celebrated career. "Miss Merman is the world's greatest salesman of lyrics," Durante later said.

Clayton, Jackson, and Durante were signed by Florenz Ziegfeld to appear in his 1929 summer production of *Show Girl*. Jimmy and Jeanne had tried to spend at least one month of each summer in the country — they cherished the log cabin and lake fishing lifestyle — but 1929 marked the beginning of the end for even these brief vacations together, and Jeanne's physical condition grew increasingly worse.

Show Girl premiered in Boston. Appearing along with Clayton, Jackson, and Durante were Frank McHugh, Eddie Foy, and Ruby Keeler, who was then married to Al Jolson. On opening night, Jolson ran down the aisle and sang a song with his wife, much to the delight of the full house. The show moved to New York in July and received superlative reviews that devoted the most attention to Durante. The overflowing, cheering audiences kept coming until October when *Show Girl* closed as all Broadway business fell with the coming of the Depression.

While preparing to go back to nightclub work, Lou Clayton was contacted by Paramount Pictures. Playwrights Ben Hecht and Charles MacArthur had recommended their friends Clayton, Jackson, and Durante for roles in the movie *Roadhouse Nights* (1929), also starring Helen Morgan, Charles Ruggles, and Fred Kohler. It was Durante's first movie and his first billing as "The Schnozzola."

Clayton, Jackson, and Durante were paid $50,000 for four weeks of shooting. Paramount had a filming lot on Long Island, which allowed the comedy team to perform three shows daily in New York City while making the movie. (The Palace had booked them again, and they also played a late-night show at the Silver Slipper club.) *Photoplay* reviewed *Roadhouse Nights*: "Jimmy Durante is immense in the Roadhouse sequence. Watch this Durante!"

During November 1929, each of the three entertainers was earning $20,000 — in a country in the midst of an economic collapse.

In early autumn of 1930, Clayton, Jackson, and Durante were signed with Hope Williams, Ann Pennington, Frances Williams, and Charles King to star in E. Ray Goetz's stage production *The New Yorkers*, with music by Cole Porter. A re-write of work inserted, among other things, the "wood number" into the first act. Clayton, Jackson, and Durante stole the show, but *The New Yorkers* was their final professional engagement as a comedy team.

Durante with groceries for the unemployed during the Depression.

On to Hollywood

Betty Furness and friend welcome Durante to Hollywood, 1930.

Durante had received earlier offers to perform solo, but had not wanted to "go back on me pals." This time, however, when MGM offered him a five-year contract of at least two movies a year, his friends strongly urged him to accept. Clayton said, "We want you to be the success you deserve . . . I'll be your manager and Eddie will work backstage." Clayton arranged the deal, and the Durantes moved to California.

His first picture of the contract was *Get-Rich-Quick Wallingford* (1931). *Photoplay* said: "This boy Durante is knocking Hollywood for a row of dialogue writers and is going to be one of the big shots all over the country before many feet of film have passed through the camera." Unfortunately, there was very little good material around for Durante, and after the success of *Get-Rich-Quick Wallingford,* for a time Durante made only brief appearances in mediocre films; he played the pal of singer Lawrence Tibbett in *The Cuban Love Song* (1931); and he received promising reviews in Buster Keaton's *The Passionate Plumber* (1932) and *Speak Easily* (1932). But the films themselves were critical and box-office disasters. *The Wet Parade* (1932) was an exception. This entertaining film starred Robert Young; Jimmy played Abe Schilling, a Prohibition agent.

Durante in The Cuban Love Song *(1931), sings his famous "I Ups to Him."*

Durante clowning between scenes of The Cuban Love Song *(1931).*

(Left to right) *Oliver Hardy, Stan Laurel,
Jimmy Durante, and Buster Keaton, early 1930s.*

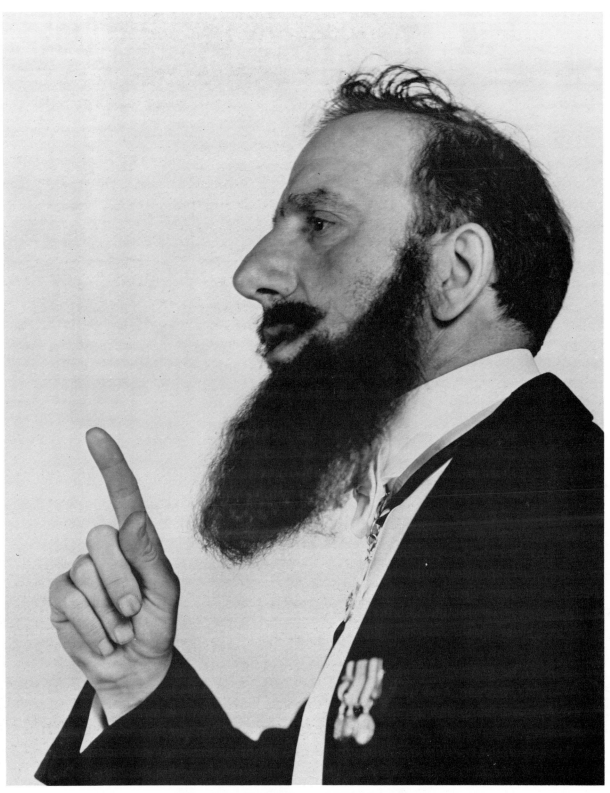

Durante as Abe Schilling in MGM's The Wet Parade *(1932).*

Right: Durante and Robert Young (left) between scenes of The Wet Parade *(1932).*

Below: Durante with Mr. and Mrs. Joe E. Brown at a movie premiere, 1932.

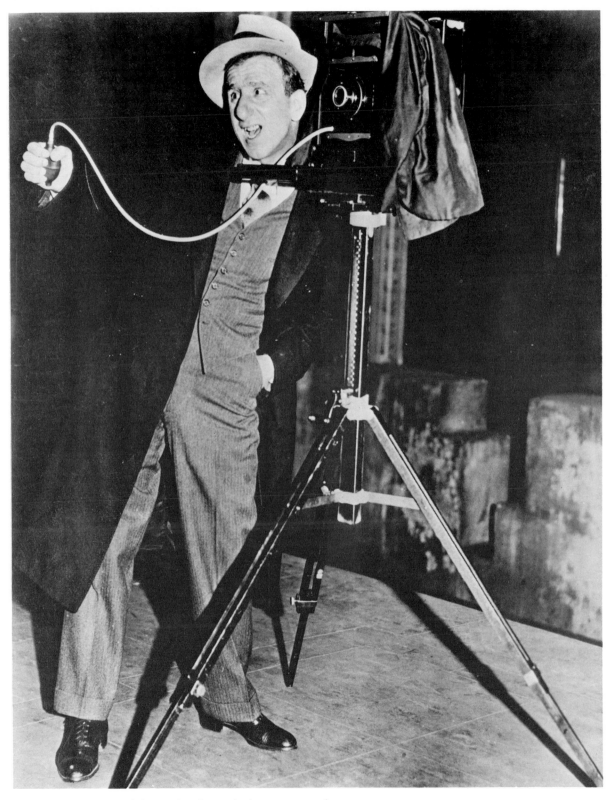

*Durante in New York hamming it up during a personal appearance tour
to promote* The Wet Parade *in 1932.*

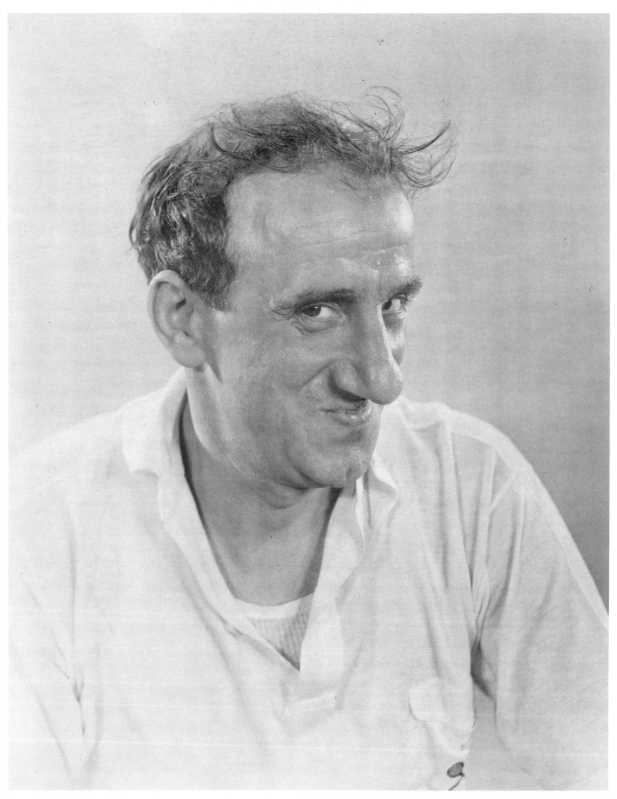

Publicity photo for Speak Easily *(1932).*

With friend Mrs. Richard Bathelmess at a party in honor of
actress Marion Davies, October 1931.

With Ginger Rogers, 1931.

*Left: Durante with Colleen More
and Robert Montgomery in
the early 1930s.*

*Below: Durante and friend Polly
Moran on the MGM lot,
early 1930s.*

Durante relaxing at home, December 1931.

The Phantom President (1932), with Claudette Colbert, was George M. Cohan's first and last Hollywood effort. The movie was a political satire about a traveling medicine man who looks like one of the major parties' candidate for President. Cohan was treated with little respect by the film industry and even before filming began on this his only screen effort, he wanted to abandon the project. Lou Clayton recalled overhearing George M. speaking to Durante: ''Jimmy, I love you. If it was anybody else in this picture but you, I'd throw up the job. But I want you to walk away with this picture. This racket out here isn't my business. I don't know why they wanted me to come out here in the first place, or why I was ever dumb enough to come. But I want you to walk away with this picture, Jim, because I love the ground you walk on.''

''Aw, gee, George,'' said Durante, ''you got me all flustered up. I don't know how to suppress it in words.''

Durante and Clark Gable
at a movie premiere in 1932.

Durante with director Norman Taurog and a blackfaced George M. Cohan, early 1930s.

Bing Crosby and Durante in The Phantom President *(1932).*

Marion Davies hugs Durante in Blondie of the Follies *(1932) to the delight of onlookers.*

The New York Times review of *Blondie of the Follies* (1932), with Marion Davies, describes Jimmy's limited role in the film: "Durante pops in irrelevantly for three minutes or so which is long enough for him to break up the show. He sings one of his 'disa and data' songs, heaps vigorous and naughty scorn on his imaginary enemies and does a mad impression of John Barrymore in which Marion Davies figures as Greta Garbo."

At a party honoring Marion Davies, October 1931.

Right: Publicity photo, 1932.

Below: Durante with Hoot Gibson, his wife Sally Eilers, and Marion Nixon in 1932.

*With Maurice Chevalier
in the early 1930s.*

With Clark Gable in the early 1930s.

(Left to right) *Oliver Hardy, Jimmy Durante, and Stan Laurel in 1932.*

With Mr. and Mrs. Tom Mix in 1932.

Durante also appeared briefly in *What! No Beer?* (1933), *Hell Below* (1933), and *Meet the Baron* (1933). He also traveled between New York and Hollywood several times to make personal appearances at movie theaters and to be on radio for the first time. He then signed for a Broadway musical comedy, *Strike Me Pink*.

Strike Me Pink (1933) played for just over 100 performances on Broadway. The musical bombed with the reviewers, but Durante held his own. Although the team of Clayton, Jackson, and Durante no longer existed as performers, Durante's salary of $3,000 a week was split three ways between his partners. Eddie Jackson, who had accompanied Durante to California, would soon rejoin the East Coast nightclub circuit and performed with Durante when Jimmy returned to nightclub work. Lou Clayton stayed with Jimmy as his business manager until Clayton's death in 1950. But in 1933, "The Three Sawdust Bums" were already looking back at their vaudeville years together as "the good old days."

In What! No Beer? *(1933).*

Publicity photo for What! No Beer? *(1933).*

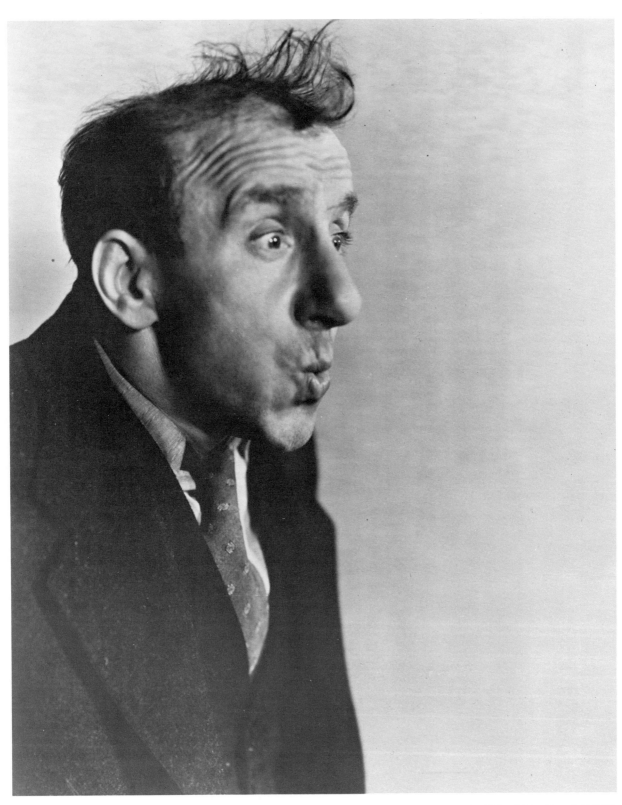

In What! No Beer? *(1933).*

At the Paradise Club in New York with Jack Dempsey (also kneeling) and others in celebration of the return of 3.2 beer, April 1933.

As Durante boards a train
in Los Angeles to go to
New York, he flashes
''Pose #3: The Full
Poisonality'' to his fans,
February 1933.

Durante and wife, Jeanne,
arrive in New York,
February 1933.

Trying a double shot during an MGM golf tournament, July 1932.

The Durantes with Harold Lloyd at a sporting event in New York, February 1933.

*Jimmy and Jeanne in Santa Monica, California,
with Roscoe Ates and his daughter Dorothy, August 1933.*

Laying flowers at Greta Garbo's dressing room door, February 1933.

*Greta Garbo and Jimmy Durante marionettes as they appeared
in a museum exhibit, July 1933.*

*Publicity photo,
September 1933.*

*With the aid of trick
photography, two dis-
tinctive ''schnozzolas''
change places for this 1933
publicity photo.*

June 1933.

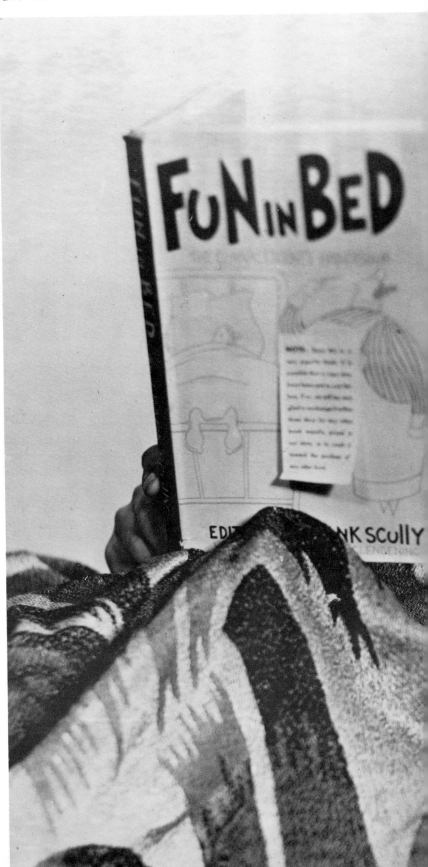

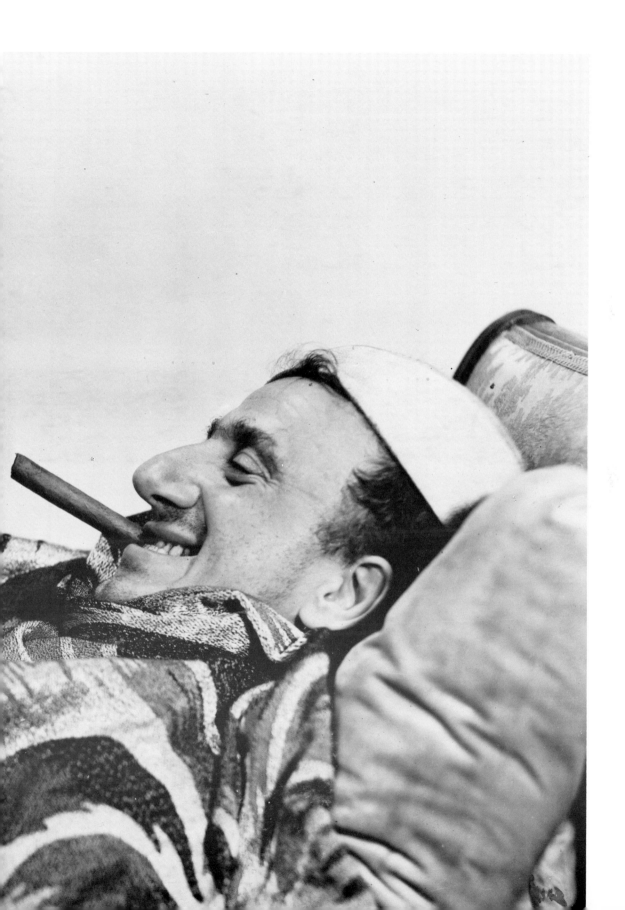

*Right: Publicity photo,
September 1933.*

*Below: The Durantes at the
Beverly Wilshire Hotel, Beverly
Hills, California, 1933.*

With Spanky MacFarland of the Little Rascals on the MGM lot, October 1933.

(Left to right) *Ruby Keeler (Mrs. Al Jolson), Jeanne Durante, Al Jolson, and Jimmy Durante during a Palm Springs, California, vacation in November 1933.*

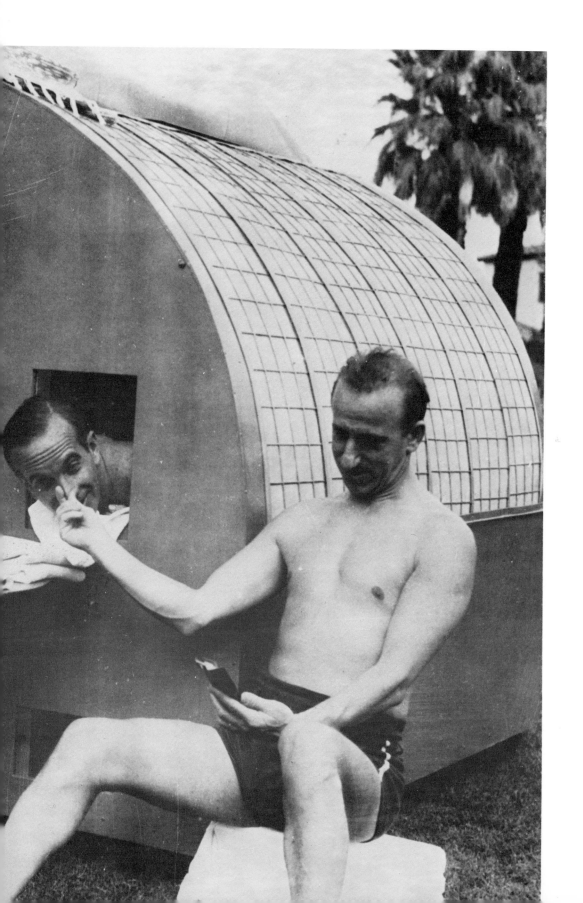

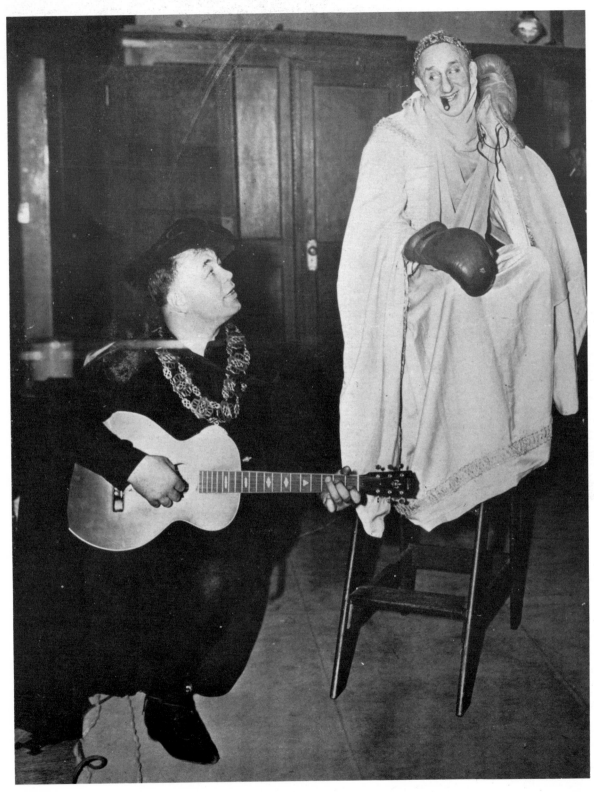

With Tony Galento in the 1930s.

Receiving a music lesson from Abe Lyman at the Cocoanut Grove
in Los Angeles, December 1933.

With Lupe Velez in the early 1930s.

With (left to right) Jean Parker, Ruth Channing,
and Irene Hervey at MGM, 1933.

With Robert Montgomery at a movie premiere, early 1930s.

With Bill Robinson (''Mr. Bojangles''), 1933.

*Publicity photo
for* Palooka *(1934).*

Back in Hollywood, Jimmy played fight manager Knobby Walsh in United Artists'
Palooka (1934). In it he performed what was to become his theme song, "Inka Dinka
Doo," a song he wrote with pianist Harry Donnelly. (It is interesting to note that few
people ever sing any songs written by Durante. "Today when a songwriter sees me on da
street, he runs. Why, if I had been the foist one to sing 'Columbia da Gem a Da Ocean,'
dat woulda been da last you woulda hoid of it.")

His *Palooka* appearance marked one of the few respectable parts Jimmy was given by
Hollywood. Following that, he appeared in *Hollywood Party* (1934) as Schnarzan of the
Apes, a Tarzan parody. Then he appeared in MGM's *Student Tour* (1934), RKO's *Strictly
Dynamite* (1934), Fox's film production of George White's *Scandals* (1934), and
Columbia's *Carnival* (1934). Durante's talents were wasted in each film. He would walk
into a scene, cast in an insignificant role, do a piece of business, and walk off.

Durante did receive permission from MGM to sign a 26-week, $130,000 contract with
the "Chase and Sanborn Radio Coffee Hour," but the motion picture industry itself was
stripping Durante of the enormous popular appeal he had worked so hard to establish for
himself. Lou Clayton began to seek stage work for him. Movies were doing Jimmy
no good.

In Palooka *(1934).*

In Palooka *(1934).*

Arriving in Hollywood to appear in MGM's Hollywood Party *(1934).*

Durante, as Schnarzan, and Lupe Velez in Hollywood Party *(1934).*

In Hollywood Party *(1934).*

Publicity photo for Hollywood Party *(1934).*

In Hollywood Party *(1934) with Polly Moran.*

In Hollywood Party (1934) with Lupe Velez.

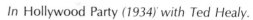
In Hollywood Party (1934) with Ted Healy.

*Left: With Charles Butterworth
in a publicity photo for*
Student Tour *(1934).*

Below: With Alice White in
Strictly Dynamite *(1934).*

Right: Between scenes of Scandals (1934) with Dixie Dunbar and Cliff Edwards.

Below: Durante, as Best Man, watches as the characters played by Rudy Vallee and Alice Faye are married in Scandals (1934).

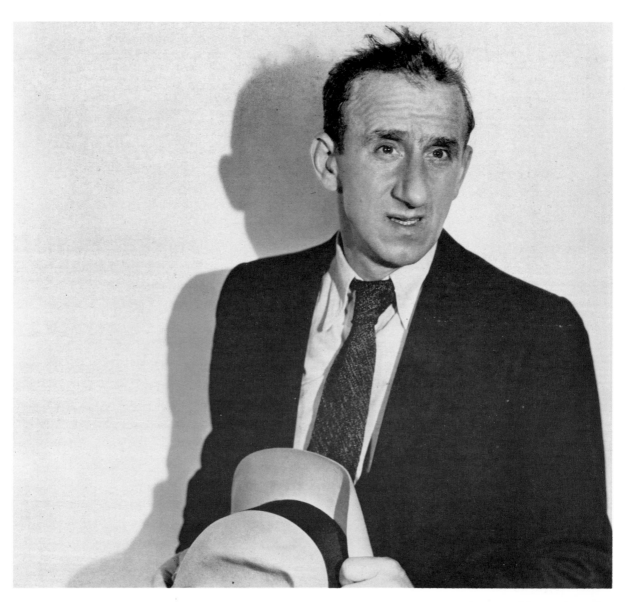

Above: Publicity photo for
Scandals *(1934).*

Right: With Eunice Coleman
between scenes of Scandals *(1934).*

Above: Lee Tracy and Durante clowning at Columbia studios, 1934.

Right: Durante breaking in a new piano — ''pianner bustin','' as he calls it, June 1934.

In Strictly
Dynamite *(1934).*

Clowning around the back lot at RKO, 1934.

*With Ed Wynn,
mid-1930s.*

*(Left to right) Robert Vignola, ''Papa'' Bartolomeo Durante, Jeanne Durante, Ida Korverman,
and Jimmy Durante at a Hollywood premiere, 1934.*

On vacation in Palm Springs, California, in 1934.

Right: MGM publicity photo, 1934.

Below: With Baby Rose Marie at a New Year's party, December 31, 1934.

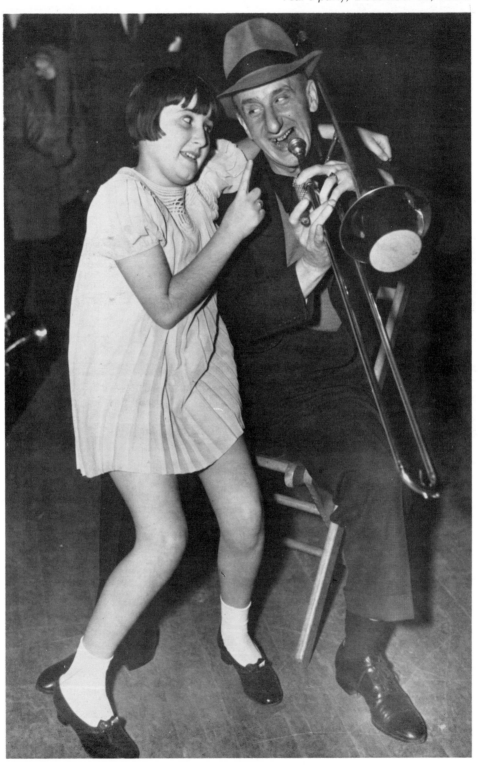

Friends Ben Hecht and Charles MacArthur had a new play in the works, a Billy Rose extravaganza called *Jumbo* with music by Rogers and Hart. Jimmy was cast as the illiterate press agent Claudius "Brainy" Bowers, a classic Durante characterization. The show opened in November 1935, at the Hippodrome in New York.

"It seems," said Durante, "that Hecht and MacArthur always showed up in time to save me from some dilemma; first with *Roadhouse Nights*; next when MacArthur gave me *Get-Rich-Quick Wallingford*; and now they concockted *Jumbo* for me. It is Hecht and MacArthur who give me lines in *Roadhouse Nights* that I'm always fond of, like, 'It's the gallows!' and 'I'm just a tool for a beautiful dame!' And I told Charlie I would play *Jumbo*.

"As for this Billy Rose, he is dynamite. He tore out the insides of the old Hippodrome and made the stage like a circus ring, right in the middle of the place, with the people sitting all around, and a circular curtain to come down on the ring. I fell in love with the whole setup."

George Abbott directed this story of a bankrupt circus owner, Mr. Considine, and his rival, Mr. Mulligan. A Romeo and Juliet romance between their son and daughter develops and tax collectors move to dispossess Mr. Considine when his circus closes. His press agent, played by Durante, intervenes to aid his troubled boss.

Jimmy was not surprised by the show's success, but remembered getting unanticipated laughs. "I am trying to steal the elephant Jumbo, and am walking along in this scene when the sheriff shouts, 'What are you doing with that elephant?' And I replies, 'What elephant?' This line got one of the biggest laughs in the show, much to my surprise!"

Jumbo ran for 233 performances before closing in April of 1936. Producer Billy Rose arranged with NBC to make *Jumbo* a continuing radio series. Durante appeared with cast members Gloria Grafton, Donald Novis, and Arthur Sinclair on Tuesday nights.

Meanwhile, Lou Clayton was working out a European tour for Durante, but before Jimmy would go, he wanted to vacation with Jeanne in Florida.

Softhearted Jimmy was a sucker for a request by anyone for money or help, and while in Miami, a hotel owner called on Durante to fill in at the Royal Palms when his contracted performer fell ill. "What a dope I was! It is a sour antidote of my life."

Jimmy stole off from his wife in the evening to perform at the Palms. She caught on quickly, of course, and confronted Jimmy at the club. "What are you trying to prove? How much punishment you can take?"

"I don't know what I'm trying to prove, Toots. I should get my head exterminated, but these fellows are pals."

"People take advantage of your friendship, Jimmy. You'll never learn."

"You know," recalled Jimmy, "when a person is sick, as Jeanne was, they're irritable, and instead of arguin' with them, if only we had the will power, we should never do it. But how many of us have got that will power, that when they say somethin', you don't try to say somethin' back? More so if you're married than you would to a friend. I don't know the difference, but when you are married, your wife says somethin' to you and it hurts you.

A New Year's Day message from Jimmy Durante.

With Jeanne at Santa Anita Racetrack in California, mid-1930s.

One word leads to another, and there you are, two fine people in a mess of words that can't be unsaid in a hurry.

"Jeanne was one of the sweetest gals in the whole world when she wasn't sick, as anyone can tell you. She was so goodhearted and good-natured. And she says, 'All right, go ahead. Go on and do the other nights.' "

The European Tour

While the Durantes took a train back to California from Florida, Lou Clayton booked Jimmy for appearances in Dublin, Liverpool, Glasgow, and London at a salary of £1,000 a week — a record sum for show business personalities of the time. Jimmy had trouble breaking the news of his new engagements to Jeanne whose condition had improved. She assumed they would be staying at home in California for some time.

"I got to thinkin' to myself. I said, 'Gee, I'm crazy bookin' like this.' Like Jeanne said, 'What am I tryin' to prove?' I know nothin' about Europe. Here we're now home again, and Jeanne is dyin' to stay put. She's happy again and feelin' a lot better, and here I've gone and booked that foreign engagement. How am I gonna break the news to her? So I'm in a condition of mental confusion."

They argued. Jeanne decided to accompany Jimmy, then changed her mind. She ended up getting on the train with her husband bound for New York and getting off in Pasadena. She returned home and wished her husband well on his European tour. Jimmy made it to New York, met Lou Clayton, then decided to return to his wife in California at the last minute. He sent his bags to the train station and prepared to go home. Clayton, however, ordered that Jimmy's bags be placed aboard the French liner *Normandie* and proceeded to "abduct" Durante to Europe.

Clayton took this and other forceful actions during Durante's career, not to hurt him or Jeanne, not for the money, but because he felt deeply that it was his responsibility to present Jimmy Durante, a brilliant artist and a superior human being, to the world. Clayton believed he had the conviction, ambition, and confidence that Durante lacked, and that Jimmy had everything else necessary to become the world's most beloved comic.

Clayton elaborated: "Jimmy's heart is in the right place, and that's what makes him understood by everybody. And when I wanted to take him abroad, I wanted the people over there to see him in the flesh and know what a good man he was. And I wasn't going to let anyone or anything stop this, even if I had to trick him into getting on the boat."

On the French liner Normandie *en route to Europe, 1936.*

Clayton arranged for a bon voyage party for some theatrical people. He had a piano brought aboard the *Normandie* and dragged Jimmy to see Max Gordon, Martin Beck, and others who were in attendance. Durante, of course, began ''playin' pianner'' and singing and didn't notice the call to go ashore. ''Lou, the boat's shakin','' Jimmy howled. ''Can't you feel the viperations? Help! We're on the brainy deep!''

The European tour (London, Liverpool, Glasgow, Paris, and Rome) was a great success. The audiences loved him and Durante was thrilled to have discovered so many friends far from home.

Left and below: After a long night of partying in Paris, Durante is delighted to read about himself in Paris-Soir, 1936.

*A characteristic
pose, August 1935.*

Before returning to California, Jimmy appeared on Broadway in *Red, Hot and Blue*, a Cole Porter musical, written by Howard Lindsay and Russel Crouse, co-starring old friend Ethel Merman and new comic talent Bob Hope. The show played 183 performances and then moved to Chicago for a six-week run. While in the Windy City, Jimmy also appeared at the Chez Paree nightclub. Then he returned to New York and worked with the vaudeville team of Long and (Danny) Kaye.

Durante was always a big horse racing fan. This shot of him was taken at one of his favorite tracks, Santa Anita in California, 1935.

Durante mugs for the camera upon his return to the U.S. after successfully touring Europe, September 1936.

*With Al Jolson (kneeling) and Eddie Cantor
during a night out on the town, 1935.*

With Bill Robinson (left) and Mayor Fiorello La Guardia at the Municipal Lodging House of New York's Thanksgiving Day dinner, November 1936.

Durante and Robinson (right) join one of the homeless guests for Thanksgiving dinner.

*With columnist Dorothy Kilgallen (left)
and Mary Lewis at the Club Versailles in New York, 1936.*

Years later, Durante fondly remembers his 1936 European tour.

The Hard Years

At last Jimmy made his way back to California. This period in Hollywood was no different from the last. He appeared in three mediocre films — *Start Cheering* (1938), *Sally, Irene, and Mary* (1938), and Shirley Temple's *Little Miss Broadway* (1938). Disgusted with the big studios, Jimmy returned to Broadway in February of 1939 to play in *Stars in Your Eyes* with Ethel Merman. The musical was well received and ran for 16 weeks at the Majestic Theatre.

Durante and three friends play "The Big Bad Wolf" and
"The Three Little Pigs" while on vacation in Palm Springs, California, 1930s.

With Fred Allen in Sally, Irene, and Mary *(1938).*

Publicity photo with Fred Allen for Sally, Irene, and Mary *(1938).*

Jimmy's career was on the skids and a serious auto accident involving Lou Clayton did not help matters. Lou was thrown through the windshield of his car and required corrective surgery during the following three years. His medical expenses exceeded $70,000. Durante helped Lou with the bills by taking out personal loans. Jeanne sold keepsakes and valuables from her safe deposit box. The Durantes' housekeeper, Maggie Arnold, offered to work without pay. Lou was taken care of, despite the tremendous financial strain that had been imposed on the "family."

Durante then decided to spend more time with Jeanne and to reflect upon his sagging career. He called this period in his life his "lowest pernt." Already in his late forties, he was considered too old for movies, and his form of humor was considered outdated.

During this time, he appeared in Gene Autry's *Melody Ranch* (1940). "I'd never rode a horse and the horse had never been rode! We both started out on even terms. It was a catastrastroke!"

Then he went to New York with Jeanne to appear in *Keep Off the Grass*, which co-starred Ray Bolger. The musical review was a flop and the Durantes returned to California. Jimmy worked New Year's week of 1941 at a club in Hollywood for $2,500 a week, $500 below his usual minimum fee.

Then word came to Jimmy that his 93-year-old father, who was suffering from hardening of the arteries, had collapsed from a heart attack and was near death. Jimmy rushed to New York but did not arrive in time to see his father alive. Like Jimmy, Bartolomeo was in the habit of spoiling his friends. Jimmy said that several hundred mourners passed by his father's coffin.

Durante now found himself in dire financial straits, which left him no alternative but to get back to serious work. He called Eddie Jackson and drummer Jack Roth, and together they went on an old-fashioned East Coast vaudeville tour. Few people took notice, but the act did well wherever it played, and Durante reveled in the sound of applause once again. While Durante was on tour, however, tragedy struck — Jeanne was hospitalized with internal hemorrhages, and Jimmy's sister died suddenly in New York.

"My sister was the sweetest person who ever lived," Durante later said. "I don't think she ever harmed a fly. Now we're at home for the wake, and I sit up all night, and while I'm waitin' there, I get the biggest shock of my life. Who walks in but my wife, Jeanne! She had flown to New York sick as she was. She looked like a ghost. And she gets awful sick the next day.

"Oh, I thought I'd never get her back to California alive. We got home on the train, with Jeanne very sick all the way, and I take her down to Palm Springs again, and wait for phone calls to get some work to pay the bills."

Durante soon appeared in *You're in the Army Now* (1942) with Phil Silvers. Next was *The Man Who Came to Dinner* (1942) in which he played Banjo in a satire of Harpo Marx. Meanwhile, Lou Clayton was busy firming up a radio contract whereby Durante would make two appearances on the "Camel Caravan" program for $2,500 a show. Clayton had also negotiated a new MGM film contract that specified that Durante would shoot only one picture a year for five years. Lou figured that the studio would use Durante's talent more selectively that way. "And while you're in New York," Lou told Jimmy, "you'll play the Copacabana for two weeks at $3,000 a week!"

Jimmy didn't want to go. Jeanne was terminally ill now, and her end might come within those two weeks. But for the first time since the start of his career, Jeanne encouraged Jimmy to go; he did.

First he did the radio shows. The response was tremendous and Jimmy was excited to open at the Copa the following night. Early the next morning, though, Jimmy learned that Jeanne was dead. He flew to California and sat by her casket for three days and nights. "Things go through your brain. Maybe if I was there it wouldn't have happened. But thank God, she went to bed, and they said about four o'clock in the mornin' she passed away after collapsin'. And you get to thinkin' and thinkin', not only about this, but about the little farm you never got for her, a place where you could have lived together on spinach,

Father and son, March 1937.

like she used to say. And you wonder why these things never happen. Always somethin' would come up."

To Clayton he said, "I been thinkin', Lou. I've only got you left now. And if you leave me, I can't tell what I might do to myself."

"Jim, I'll leave you someday. I'm six years older than you and the day will come when I leave you for keeps. So make up your mind to that. But meanwhile, you're going right to New York and getting to work."

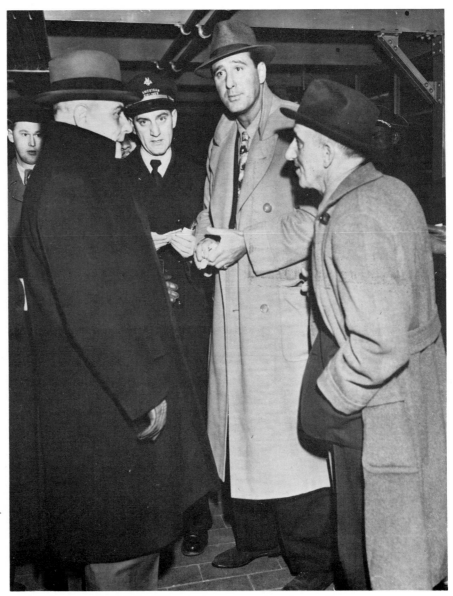

Detroit Tigers' out-fielder Hank Greenberg (center) is greeted in New York by his father (left) and friend Durante, February 1941.

(Left to right) *Cesar Romero, Tyrone Power, Durante, and John Carradine at a charity show, December 1941.*

*Above: With Marlene Dietrich (center) during a war bond drive at the
Los Angeles Victory House, February 1942.*

Right: Playing Santa Claus for the Crippled Children's Federation in New York, Christmas Day, 1942.

Above: Durante at the piano with friends including Fredric March (far right), Leslie Howard (3rd from right), Maurice Chevalier (standing, 5th from right), and Groucho Marx (with cigar).

Left: With Monty Woolley (left) and Ann Sheridan in The Man Who Came to Dinner *(1942).*

Durante returned to the Copacabana and was held over for 14 weeks. ''The minute that band plays and you get out on the floor, you seem to forget everythin'. Everythin' else goes from your mind, thinkin' of your jokes. Your mind is flashin' ahead to what's goin' to come after this, and the only time anythin' ever distracts from you, if you look to the first row in a theatre or cafe and you see a guy with a puss on him, and he's lookin' at you like he hates your guts, and you haven't done nothin' to the guy, and you think of it, and it annoys you. But you don't keep lookin' at him. You're up in the air. And the band plays. And you forget even your griefs for a moment, like a shot of dope. It's the only way I can explain it. You forget everythin' until you come off. Then when you come off, you flop down.''

With Garry Moore to publicize the Moore-Durante radio show on CBS, early 1940s.

Second Wind

Durante's contract with MGM permitted him unlimited access to the other media. Clayton had soon arranged a five-year contract at $5,000 a week for Jimmy to appear on Camel's "Gary Moore Show." The program would air weekly until late in 1947 and was a successful, happy venture for both Moore and Durante. Jimmy's special talent for mispronunciation and malapropism projected beautifully over the air to a listening audience. He insisted, "I never mispernounce poipoisly. I ain't phonyin' up dem woids. It jest comes out like dat." But when Garry Moore once tried to improve Durante's diction, Jimmy warned, "You teach me to say dem woids right and we're both outa a job."

It was during the Camel radio show that Jimmy originated his famous curtain line, "Good night, Mrs. Calabash, wherever you are." The adieu was meant for Jeanne, his great love whom he never got a chance to say goodbye to in life.

Durante's success on radio proved that he was still a successful and popular entertainer. As a result, his next series of motion picture appearances showcased more of his talents.

Jimmy made a brief appearance in the film *Two Girls and a Sailor* (1944) in which he performed his "Everybody Wants to Get Inta de Act!" routine. In *Music for Millions* (1944) he introduced the crazy Irving Caesar song "Umbriago." In *Two Sisters from Boston* (1946), which co-starred June Allyson and Kathryn Grayson, Jimmy played their musician-godfather who screams at the orchestra, bangs on his piano, and badgers the chorus girls. *The New York Times* wrote after *Two Sisters*: "There is a very strong sentiment on Broadway that the Honorable James Durante is the funniest man in the world." In 1947, Jimmy played a janitor in *It Happened in Brooklyn* with Frank Sinatra. *This Time for Keeps* (1947) was an Esther Williams swim-film to which Jimmy lent a bit of lunacy.

Above: With child star Margaret O'Brien between scenes of Music for Millions *(1944).*

Right: Singing the praises of his mythical friend "Umbriago" in Music for Millions *(1944).*

With Kathryn Grayson in Two Sisters from Boston *(1946).*

On location on Mackinac Island, Michigan, for This Time for Keeps *(1947),
with Lauritz Melchior (left).*

*Durante and Melchior spend a quiet evening
at the Grand Hotel, Mackinac Island, after a long day's shooting.*

(Left to right) Durante, Jean Hersholt, and Frank Sinatra during a rehearsal for CBS Radio's "Stars in the Afternoon," October 1944.

With Margie Little at the Stork Club, New York, July 1946.

It was around this time that Jimmy met Margie Little. She was a pretty, red-haired singer-dancer who worked the East Coast resort areas. Jimmy met her in New York City and they soon began to see one another frequently.

"One night I takes her home to her hotel on 66th, and it's winter and good night at the elevator. Well, you know you try to kiss a girl, and she pushes you away? Well, I get sore. So I goes outside to call a cab, but the cab don't come, and so I walk around the block and am standin' again in front of the hotel. So all of a sudden, I hear boom! Right in front of me, a big hairbrush lands; and Margie is leanin' out a window away up above me and laughin' down. And the next day I says to her never to speak to me again.

"Then she'd be in Child's [where they used to dine] and she'd come over and say, 'Well, what do you want?' And I'd say, 'Nothin'. I want nothin'. And who the hell sent for you, anyway?' And she'd say, 'The waiter said you sent for me.' And so we make up, and she's been an awful lot of fun. Oh, we've passed some words, but most always, we've been congenital."

Celebrating his fifty-first birthday, February 1944.

(Left to right) *Betty Hutton, Durante, and Lana Turner in a publicity photo for CBS Radio's "Command Performance," 1944.*

With Mrs. Joe Pasternak (left), Faye Emerson, and Steve Crane, 1944.

Dancing with musical comedy entertainer Harriet Powell at New York's Stork Club, 1944.

With Alice Faye, 1944.

With band leader Xavier Cugat at The Waldorf Astoria, New York, 1944.

With Dinah Shore during a rehearsal for her radio show, 1944.

With orchestra leader Paul Whiteman, January 1945.

Right: With Chris Allen at the Hollywood Photographers' Ball, December 1945.

Below: (Left to right) Bert Wheeler, Jack Benny, Durante, Earl Carroll, and Errol Flynn at Carroll's restaurant, 1945.

With Duke Ellington at Hollywood's Ciro's, 1945.

Left: (Standing) *Billy Gilbert and Judy Canova;*
(sitting) *Durante and Eddie Cantor, 1945.*

*Below: With Joan Crawford at the Hollywood
Women's Press Club, January 1946.*

Durante performs with entertainer Ginny Simms on Armed Forces Radio, December 1946.

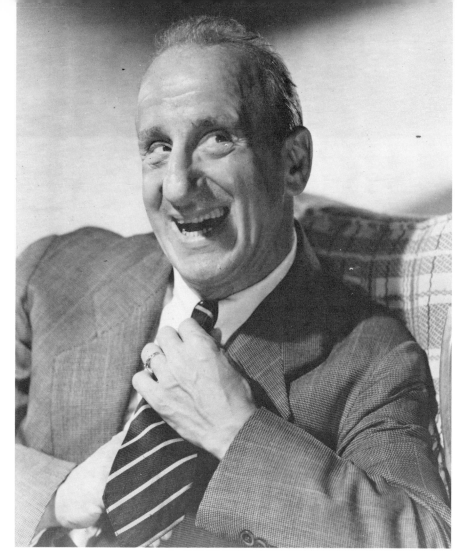

Left: MGM publicity photo, 1946.

Below: With Lassie, 1946.

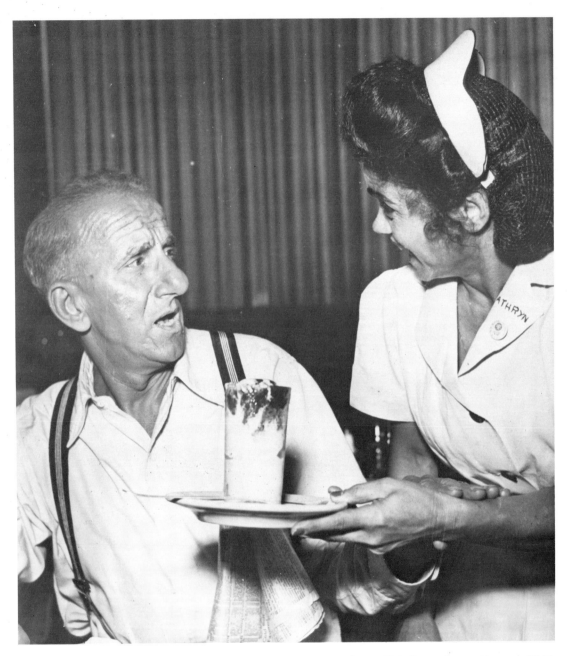

In the MGM Commissary, August 1947.

In December of 1947, Jimmy agreed to go on a charity tour for the March of Dimes. A medical exam just before he was to leave California revealed a growth on his lower intestine. Lou Clayton recalled seeing Durante crying before he went into surgery. "I'm just prayin' to God," Durante said. "It's going to be a narrow screech, I know, and I got to wonderin' what would have happened to me all these years without you fellows. I'd like to live long enough to do a little good in this world to pay back what I owe."

With Janet Leigh at a restaurant opening in Beverly Hills, California, August 1947.

Jimmy's operation was a success and he rejoiced in discovering the mail bags full of encouraging letters from fans. Red Skelton, Bob Hope, Al Jolson, and Frank Morgan had donated their services to ABC radio to fill in for Jimmy on the Durante-Moore program.

Billy Rose used the circumstance of Jimmy's ill health to reprimand the MGM studio bosses for abusing Jimmy's talent. "I hope your geniuses don't cool him off. If they can refrain from getting too clever, the greatest of our clowns should be red fire until the angels come and get him. When you cast him as a human being, rather than a jack-in-the-box specialty act, he set fire to the celluloid; but soon your hired hands were using him to prop up every crippled script on the lot. So please tell your day laborers out there that when they mess up with Jimmy they're messing with the best-loved guy in show business. If they cool him off again, strong men will come down from the mountains and up from the valleys and turn your studio into a bowling alley."

Receiving the coveted "Heart of Gold" award from singer Peggy Lee at the close of his March 10, 1948, NBC radio broadcast.

Once recovered, Durante resumed his weekly radio duties and also appeared in another Esther Williams musical *On an Island with You* (1948), in *The Great Rupert* (1950) (which concerned a performing squirrel), and in *The Milkman* (1950), in which Durante taught Donald O'Connor how to deliver milk. Durante's appearances in these films did not hurt his career, but neither did they help it. He was never challenged with having to play anyone but himself, at which he was very good, but he wasn't developing his talents any further.

At the "Heart of Gold" award dinner with Louis B. Mayer.

Van Johnson (left) and Peggy Lee guest star on Durante's radio show, March 18, 1948.

With Charles Boyer (center) and Arthur Treacher during rehearsal for Durante's radio show, April 5, 1948.

Lunching with Peggy Lee, February 1948.

Attending the funeral of Bill Robinson in New York are (left to right) New York Mayor William O'Dwyer, comedian Milton Berle, baseball star Jackie Robinson (no relation to Bill), Durante and Danny Kaye, November 28, 1949.

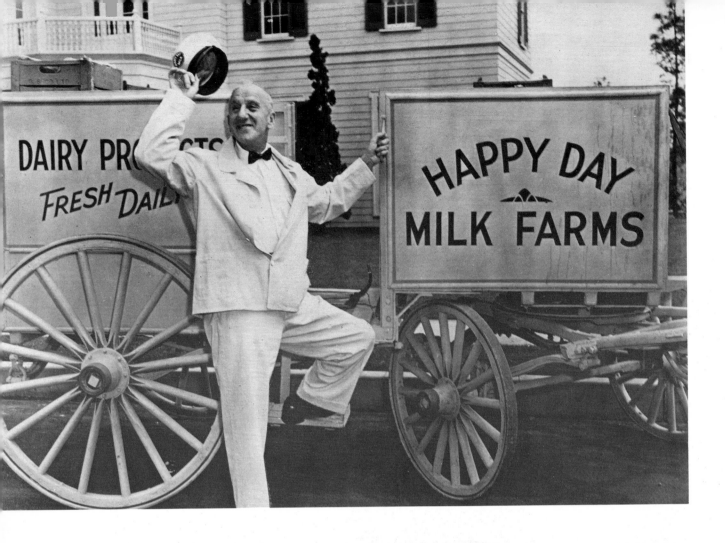

Above and right:
In The Milkman *(1950).*

With Donald O'Connor in The Milkman *(1950).*

With Donald O'Connor in The Milkman *(1950).*

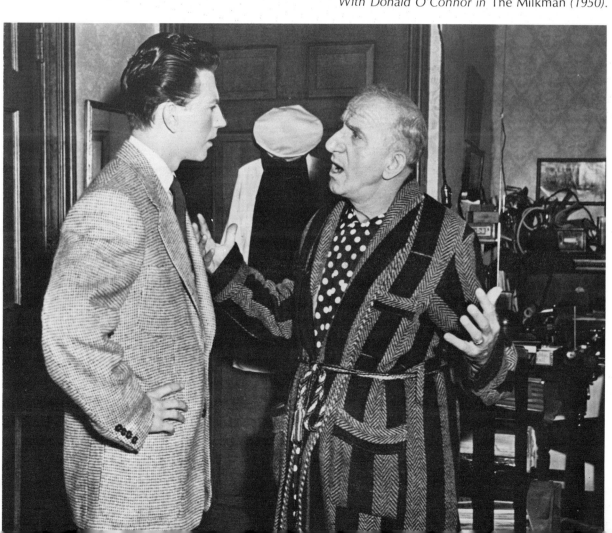

Publicity still from The Milkman *(1950) with Donald O'Connor.*

Goodbye to a Friend

Early in 1950, Lou Clayton fell seriously ill, and it was discovered that he had terminal cancer of the stomach and lower digestive tract. Initially, it was Durante's decision to keep Lou's exact condition a secret from him, however, Clayton knew that he hadn't much time left. Before he died, Lou wanted very much to secure a long-term television contract for Jimmy which would provide him with financial security.

Clayton told a writer, "I have a hunch that my number is coming up soon. And I want to raise a monument to my pal, Jimmy Durante. There's nobody as sweet as he is, or as great. In a bad world, he's stayed good. He was lucky in taking the righteous road instead of the wrong road. The crazy age that produced us sent lots of other fellows to Sing-Sing. But something inside of Jimmy Durante kept him good and honest and kind. And when you come near him, it's like warming your hands at a fire. We were only small fry, but the success of Durante, who never graduated from grade school, only goes to show you the kind of country we're living in, how beautiful it is here, and what can become of a person who hasn't got an education or doesn't take beauty prizes, but has a lovely heart."

Lou spent his last days sunning in Durante's back yard. Jimmy would go off to radio rehearsals and other jobs, and Clayton arranged for many television executives to talk with Durante about a new career. But Jimmy had no intention of moving East, which is what a long-term TV contract would have necessitated.

"It is my hope that Durante will sign up for this," said Clayton to the writer. "It means an added annual income of $200,000 for the next ten years. That would give him security. If he can't save something out of that for his old age, then to hell with him." Perhaps the major reason why Durante hesitated to relocate and pursue television was that he knew Lou would not be going with him. And without Lou, Jimmy did not see himself in show business at all.

"Take good care of the big-nosed fellow," said Clayton to Eddie Jackson and the few associates that surrounded his deathbed. "If I ever hear of anyone hurting him, I'll come down from Heaven and kill him."

*Durante tries to conceal his identifying feature from an airline employee
upon arrival in New York, April 1952.*

Jimmy stayed home for several weeks following Clayton's death, then he emerged to announce that he would accept an NBC offer and travel East to do television shows. "I'm only doin' it because Lou would have wanted it that way . . . As for me, I'd like to stay right here in California. For now without Lou, it's like I've lost both my arms and legs."

Jimmy made his television debut in October 1950. His co-star was Donald O'Connor. New York *Herald Tribune* columnist John Crosby wrote: "I think — choosing my words as carefully as possible here and after due consultation with our Restraint Department — that it was the best show I ever saw on television."

After just one season on the air, Durante was presented with the George Foster Peabody award as television's best performer of the year. "I rubbed elbows with scientists and educators. Dey wouldn't shake hands wit' me, so I rubbed elbows wid 'em!" In 1952, he won an Emmy Award as the Best Comedian of that year.

Left: With William Frawley, early 1950s.

Below: During a rehearsal for his television show with Bette Davis, April 19, 1952.

*A combined total of 130 years in show business: (left to right) Durante,
Sophie Tucker, and Eddie Jackson, December 1952.*

Publicity photo, 1956.

Durante's shows boasted the finest talent available and put performers such as opera star Helen Traubel and actor John Wayne into uproarious comedic situations. Wayne later recalled, ''Jimmy has a habit of throwing me cues for the second sketch. Except it's still the first sketch. If it had been anyone else, I would have walked off the stage. But I love the guy so, I just stood there looking silly.''

Durante made an unbilled appearance in a Bob Hope film, *Beau James* (1957), and that same year he received a standing ovation from the United States Senate when he was observed in the visitors' gallery among a group of tourists. On December 14, 1960, 67-year-old Jimmy married Margie Little.

''Jimmy didn't sweep me off my feet at first. He came to my apartment after work one night with a record album under his arm. He was no sooner through the door when he turned down the lights and started the phonograph. 'What's this?' I asked shyly. 'One of my pals has been telling me a fella should have soft lights and sweet music when he goes callin',' said Jimmy. I was touched. Suddenly, Jimmy's 'sweet music' almost blasted me out of my chair as the phonograph gave forth with Al Jolson singing 'Swanee.' ''

''It was touch and go all the way to the alter,'' Margie said later. ''They almost wouldn't give us a license because Jimmy had left the blood test certificates in his hotel room.'' (In 1961, the Durantes adopted an infant girl, Cecilia Alicia — Ceci for short.)

Right: With Margie Little, June 1949.

Below: With Margie at New York's Stork Club, December 1950.

Departing for Europe aboard the Queen Elizabeth *with fiancée Margie, April 1952.*

Arriving in New York with Margie, 1957.

*Eddie Jackson and Durante
performing together during
a tribute to Durante,
March 17, 1957.*

Right: Eddie Jackson honors his old friend.

Below: Tallulah Bankhead, Edward G. Robinson, and Danny Kaye were also on hand to pay tribute to Durante . . .

. . . as were George Jessel and Sophie Tucker.

With friend Robert Mitchum, late 1950s.

Jimmy appeared briefly in the film *Pepe* (1960) and in an Italian feature *Giudizio Universale* (1961). In 1962, he co-starred with Stephen Boyd, Doris Day, and Martha Raye in MGM's movie version of *Jumbo*. His touching film performance endeared him even more to his public than the stage version had. During this time, Jimmy also made infrequent nightclub appearances with Eddie Jackson. They worked occasional one-week stands in New York, Miami, and San Juan. Durante then worked in Stanley Kramer's star-studded motion picture *It's A Mad, Mad, Mad, Mad World* (1963). Jimmy played Smiler Grogan, an old man who dies and literally "kicks the bucket."

In 1966, Jimmy made a guest appearance on Lucille Ball's situation comedy television show. In November of that year, he played Humpty Dumpty in television's version of *Alice Through the Looking Glass*, and as a favor to Bob Hope, he appeared in one of the comedian's "Chrysler Theatre" episodes.

Left: With Martha Raye in Jumbo *(1962).*

Below: (Left to right) Doris Day, Stephen Boyd, Durante, and Martha Raye in Jumbo *(1962).*

Above: (Left to right) Jonathan Winters, Durante, Milton Berle, Mickey Rooney, Sid Caesar, and Buddy Hackett in It's A Mad, Mad, Mad, Mad World *(1963).*

Right: As Smiler Grogan in . . . Mad, Mad World *(1963).*

Entertaining patients at Walter Reed Army Medical Center, Washington, D.C., July 19, 1957.

Durante had all but retired by 1966. He was 70 years old, well-to-do, and exhausted after a long, extraordinarily varied and active career. Good friend Desi Arnaz persuaded Jimmy to appear on his "Mothers-in-Law" television series in 1969. In 1970, he co-starred with the Lennon Sisters in a television mini-series that was well received. In 1971, Durante narrated "Frosty the Snowman," an animated television special.

By 1976, Durante had suffered several debilitating strokes. He continued to be alert, but was confined to a wheelchair. For his 83rd birthday, over 800 people filled the banquet hall at the Beverly Hilton Hotel. The event raised more than $100,000 for the Jimmy Durante Pavilion of the Villa Scabrini Home for the Aged in California. On January 29, 1980, just before his 87th birthday, the beloved entertainer fell into a coma and died.

In Retrospect

Eddie Cantor, about his good friend: "When I was in the hospital with a heart attack, Jimmy came every day. I was allowed no visitors and he knew that, but he came every day and sat in the corridor outside my room."

Steve Allen: "It was 1949 and I was more or less an unknown. Some newspaper photographers asked us to pose for some pictures signing autographs for a horde of teenagers . . . [who] shouldered me out of the way. Suddenly, just as the flash bulbs were about to pop, Jim looked up. '*Wait* a minute,' he said in that characteristic way. Grabbing my arm, he pulled me in close to him. Then, satisfied, he gave the photographers the okay to shoot. That's the kind of man Durante [was]."

Perhaps Bob Hope's eulogy best sums up the life of Jimmy Durante: "When Jimmy was around, everybody started each day with a song and more importantly, with a smile. Professionally and personally Jimmy was a success. A success by every definition of the word, but especially by his own definition: 'Success is not to worry too much, to do the best you can, stick to your friends and pray they'll stick to you, and let God take care of the rest.' Well, success can be measured by the friends one has. And believe me, Jimmy Durante was the most successful man I know of."

Appearing with Bob Hope on CBS Radio's "Command Performance," 1944.

*With long-time partner
Eddie Jackson in 1956.*

Right: From the New York World-Telegram, *Saturday, April 11, 1936.*

Below: With Ed Wynn (left) and Jack Pearl on the MGM lot, 1930s.

World-Telegram Staff Photos.

"Hot'cha. . . . Feel that trusty driver. . . . This is my year, boys," says Schnozzle Durante, Jumbo of the trap-bound duffers. . . . His heart beats fast as he vows to break 100. . . .

. . . "What," queries Jimmy, "only 400 yards? Maybe I oughta use my backspin mashie. . . ."

"I'll moider it. Right foot here. . . . Left foot there. . . . Arm stiff. . . . Oooh, how sorry I feel for this ball! . . . What's the course record, buddy?

"FORE. . . . Hey, look out there! . . . I can't see the ball. . . . It must be in the next county. . . . What a wallop! . . . Aaaah, this is a game for MEN."

"The doity double-crosser . . . the lowbrow. . . . Imagin' that club! . . . An' me an embryo champ. . . . Take that, you backslider! . . . It's the same darned game."

Enjoying the beach next to Agua Caliente Racetrack, Tijuana, Mexico, August 1934.

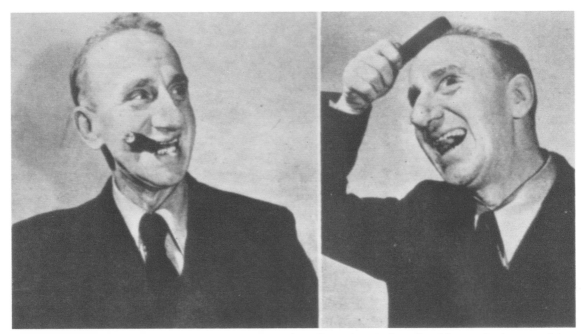

Look at *dat*. De waiter soives de sucker six olives in uh bowl of ice an' charges him twelve bucks. Ice, ice — *nuttin'* but ice. What a spot fer *Admiral Boid tuh discovah!* . . . De hair? Why dat's de way *she* wants me tuh comb it!

So I ups tuh him. He ups tuh me. I feints wit' muh right. I feints wit' muh left. I sees an openin'. I swings — *I'm flat on muh back!* . . . Break it up waiters, *break* it up. Every time two of youse congregate, *dere's a strike*.

You can't toin yer back for uh minute in dis dump — de guy dat looks like uh bum, *he's de boss!* . . . Lemme hear de band. Now lemme hear dem violins. *One violin*! Dey spare *no* expense . . . Why it's *mutiny*, dat's what it is, *mutiny!*

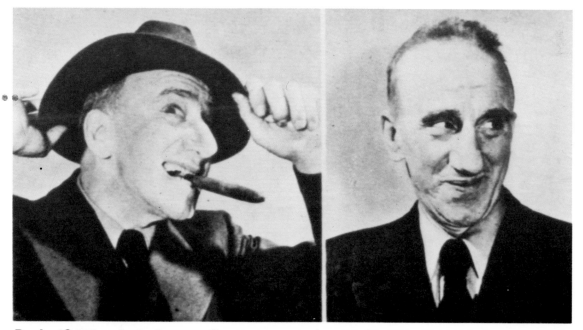

De hat? Why dat's de way *she* wants me tuh wear it. Say, what am I, anyway, uh *man* or uh *peacock?* . . . So dere I am, see, standin' in front of de joint, mindin' muh business, when dis guy walks up — *an' hitches his horse to me!*

END

Films of Jimmy Durante

Roadhouse Nights 1929 (Paramount)
Get-Rich-Quick Wallingford 1931 (MGM)
The Cuban Love Song 1931 (MGM)
The Passionate Plumber 1932 (MGM)
Speak Easily 1932 (MGM)
The Wet Parade 1932 (MGM)
The Phantom President 1932 (Paramount)
Blondie of the Follies 1932 (MGM)
What! No Beer? 1933 (MGM)
Hell Below 1933 (MGM)
Broadway to Hollywood 1933 (MGM)
Meet the Baron 1933 (MGM)
Palooka 1934 (United Artists)
Hollywood Party 1934 (MGM)
Student Tour 1934 (MGM)
Strictly Dynamite 1934 (RKO)
Scandals 1934 (Fox)
Carnival 1934 (Columbia)
Land Without Music [Forbidden Music]
   1936 (British)
Start Cheering 1938 (Columbia)

Sally, Irene, and Mary 1938 (Twentieth
   Century-Fox)
Little Miss Broadway 1938 (Twentieth
   Century-Fox)
Melody Ranch 1940 (Republic)
Your're in the Army Now 1942
   (Warner Bros.)
The Man Who Came To Dinner 1942
   (Warner Bros.)
Two Girls and a Sailor 1944 (MGM)
Music for Millions 1944 (MGM)
Two Sisters from Boston 1946 (MGM)
It Happened in Brooklyn 1947 (MGM)
This Time for Keeps 1947 (MGM)
On an Island with You 1948 (MGM)
The Great Rupert 1950 (Eagle Lion)
The Milkman 1950 (Universal)
Beau James 1957 (Paramount)
Pepe 1960 (Columbia)
Giudizio Universale 1961 (Italian)
Jumbo 1962 (MGM)

It's a Mad, Mad, Mad, Mad World 1963 (United Artists)